CASE STUDIES IN

CULTURAL ANTHROPOLOGY

GENERAL EDITORS

George and Louise Spindler

STANFORD UNIVERSITY

THE DOBE !KUNG

THE DOBE !KUNG

By

RICHARD B. LEE

University of Toronto

HOLT, RINEHART AND WINSTON

NEW YORK   CHICAGO   SAN FRANCISCO   PHILADELPHIA
MONTREAL   TORONTO   LONDON   SYDNEY   TOKYO
MEXICO CITY   RIO DE JANEIRO   MADRID

Credit: Extracts used from Richard B. Lee, *The !Kung San: Men, Women, and Work in a Foraging Society* with the kind permission of Cambridge University Press. Copyright © 1979 by Cambridge University Press.

Library of Congress Cataloging in Publication Data

Lee, Richard B.
  The Dobe !Kung.

  (Case studies in anthropology)
  Filmography: p. 161
  Bibliography: p. 165
  Includes index.
  1. !Kung (African people)   2. San (African people)
I. Title.   II. Series.
DT797.L42   1984   306'.089961   83–12916

ISBN 0-03-063803-8

Copyright © 1984 by CBS College Publishing
Address correspondence to:
383 Madison Avenue
New York, N.Y. 10017

CBS COLLEGE PUBLISHING
Holt, Rinehart and Winston
The Dryden Press
Saunders College Publishing

Foreword

ABOUT THE SERIES

These case studies in cultural anthropology are designed to bring to students, in beginning and intermediate courses in the social sciences, insights into the richness and complexity of human life, as it is lived in different ways and in different places. They are written by men and women who have lived in the societies they write about, and who are professionally trained as observers and interpreters of human behavior. The authors are also teachers, and in writing their books they have kept the students who will read them foremost in their minds. It is our belief that when an understanding of ways of life very different from one's own is gained, abstractions and generalizations about social structure, cultural values, subsistence techniques, and the other universal categories of human social behavior become meaningful.

ABOUT THE AUTHOR

Richard Lee was born in New York City in 1937 and grew up in Toronto, Canada, where he was educated in the Toronto school system. At the University of Toronto he studied anthropology, philosophy, and sciences, receiving his B.A. in 1959 and his M.A. in 1961. Moving to the University of California at Berkeley, he then studied with Sherwood Washburn, J. Desmond Clark, and Robert Murphy and, in collaboration with Irven DeVore, embarked on a doctoral study of the !Kung San of Botswana.

With DeVore he is the cofounder of the Kalahari Research Group, an informal consortium of scientists from a number of fields who have done research with the San. Lee's own trips to the !Kung between 1963 and 1983 have totaled about forty months of fieldwork.

He has taught at Harvard, Rutgers, and Columbia, and since 1972 has been a professor of anthropology at the University of Toronto. His books include *Man the Hunter* and *Kalahari Hunter-Gatherers* (with Irven DeVore), *Politics and History in Band Societies* (with Eleanor Leacock), and *The !Kung San: Men, Women, and Work in a Foraging Society.* Lee has also done ethnographic filming with the British and Canadian Broadcasting Corporations.

In addition to his work on foraging peoples, Lee has written on the political struggles of indigenous peoples, the CETI Problem, and social evolutionary theory. He is currently researching the history and evolution of early states. Dr. Lee is also active in the civil and human rights movements. He has three children, all of whom have been adopted into the !Kung kinship system.

ABOUT THIS CASE STUDY

This is a case study of the !Kung San, foragers of the Dobe area of the Kalahari Desert of northwestern Botswana, near the border of Namibia. This location is important because the Kalahari and its relative isolation provided an environment, over millenia, that nourished a significant foraging culture and insulated it from heavy penetration and influence by the outside world. In the early 1960s, Richard Lee encountered at the Dobe waterhole a group of !Kung who were living almost entirely by hunting and gathering. This made it possible for him to study the !Kung foraging adaptation, one critically important in human evolution, as a whole and intact way of life. Unlike many studies by cultural anthropologists, Lee's study was broadly oriented, including environment, resources, subsistence techniques, ecology, and ethnoarcheology, as well as kinship, marriage, social control, ritual, and belief systems. This combination of interests produces an unusually satisfying case study in which the material and ideational dimensions of !Kung life are integrated.

The profile of !Kung San culture that emerges as the case study proceeds is compelling and challenging. A picture of steady work, steady leisure, and adequate diet challenges our conceptions of Western industrialized culture as the pinnacle of human success. The traditional !Kung need to work at foraging only a few hours a day to maintain a caloric level that enables them to live vigorous lives without losing weight. And many of their waking hours are devoted to celebrating their existence through ritual and dance, as well as in leisurely and rewarding social interaction. The image of "primitive" man as grubbing an existence from a stingy environment, beset by hungry predators, living a mean, brutish, and short life, is laughably off the mark in the case of the !Kung, and we know enough about other foragers, who lived in different styles and environments, to know that it is far from the truth for most foragers, including our ancestors.

Why, then, should the new generations of !Kung want manufactured clothing, transistor radios, cattle to keep and exploit, money, jobs, alcohol, and transportation. And why should they accept the assorted ills of civilization that come with these things? Lee devotes several chapters to recent change. Across the border in Namibia, the picture is dismal. Drunkenness, homicide, venereal disease, disorder, loss of pride and identity, are dominant features of the reaction to the impact of Western industrialized culture—as they are in most places in the world where tribal peoples have suffered the impact of Western culture, technology, economics, and power.

In the Dobe area of Botswana, the !Kung San are more isolated; change is slower, and the attractive features of the traditional way of life are still evident. And, as in other places where changes have been destructive, there are significant movements back to a more traditional life pattern. Some groups of Namibian !Kung are returning to the Kalahari to forage, though they retain some contacts with Western medicine and material culture that are useful to them.

This case study is outstanding not only for its subject matter but for its style. At times technical (but never dry), at times expressive, it tries to let the people speak for themselves. Complex matters are often presented through dialogue with principal !Kung characters, so that the meaning of things to them is made clear at the same time that important technical points are made to come alive. Even kinship, that topic so beloved by professional anthropologists, and such anathema to many undergraduate students, becomes interesting. It is a game that the !Kung play to keep some order in interpersonal relationships, inheritance, marriage, and the like. It is not cut and dried, hard and fast, as it often seems to be in the literature. Marriage, sex, social interactions, cooperation, and feuding become personal, meaningful events, beyond normative rules for behavior, yet ordered by them.

Another very useful feature of this case study is its annotated list of the large number of excellent films on the !Kung, many of which are keyed into the text.

The fieldwork and long experience upon which this case study is based are respected in professional anthropological circles. We are fortunate to have a case study of the !Kung San based upon Lee's work and presented in such a fashion that we can all, whether professional anthropologists or beginning students, enjoy and be instructed by it.

GEORGE AND LOUISE SPINDLER
General editors

Calistoga, California

Preface

This is a book about the !Kung San, a remarkable people whom I have been privileged to know since the 1960s. It describes their ways of making a living, their social organization, their politics, sexual and nonsexual, and their worldview and religious beliefs.

What it can only suggest to the reader is the !Kung spirit: that peculiar combination of humor and malice, of anger and fun that characterizes their sense of themselves as a special people. These are elusive qualities, and I can only hope you catch a glimpse of them here and there, in between the more concrete accounts of work effort, caloric intake, marriage patterns, and kinship behavior.

A book like this one can also only hint at the fragility of this quality of life as it attempts to adapt in the face of onrushing change. Working with a people like the !Kung is like a race against time: only four years after my arrival the first trading store opened, six years later a school and a clinic were built. By the 1980s, transistor radios and Western clothing were everywhere. I was able to observe a foraging mode of life during the last decades of its existence. If our work had begun in 1983 instead of 1963, we would not have seen daily hunting with poisoned arrows, full-time gathering of the rich mongongo harvest, and weekly healing dances in which powerful healers spiritually defended the !Kung against illness and misfortune. Today, bow-and-arrow hunting has almost ceased, cultivated grains are now the staples of the diet, and penicillin, not n/um, is the main defense against illness. Livestock, cash reserves, and material wealth have replaced social relationships as the main source of security for the !Kung. Game meat, once freely given, is now bought and sold.

And yet, even today much remains: a vital culture, a language with over 15,000 speakers, and a people with a continuing sense of humor and self-esteem. The !Kung, in a word, are survivors, not in the pejorative sense of relics from the distant past, but in the best modern sense—a physically hardy people with inner resources of spirit. They still retain a healthy skepticism about the good intentions of those outsiders who would "develop" them, and, as of this writing, have not forgotten how to hunt and gather. If the rest of us went away tomorrow they would be none the worse for it.

/Twi!gum, a thoughtful !Kangwa man with a keen sense of the absurd, put it all into perspective. Seeing that every !Kung household owned or had access to a store-bought iron cooking pot, I recently asked /Twi, "What did the !Kung do in the old days before they had iron cooking pots to cook in?" /Twi looked at me gravely and pondered my question. After a long, meaningful silence, he finally replied, "Every-

ix

one knows that people can't live without iron cooking pots, so we must have died."

It is to /Twi, his wife N!uhka, and the !Kung of the twenty-first century that I dedicate this book.

R.B.L.

Toronto, Canada

Acknowledgments

The !Kung research was conceived at the University of California at Berkeley, was centered for many years at Harvard University, and since 1972 has branched out to a number of different institutions. I am particularly indebted to the University of Toronto for the continuing support it has provided in innumerable ways. Funding for the research has come from several sources: the National Science Foundation, the National Institute of Health, the Wenner-Gren Foundation, the Canada Council, the Social Sciences and Humanities Research Council of Canada, and the Connaught Fund of the University of Toronto. Part of this manuscript was produced during my tenure as a Connaught Senior Fellow in the Social Sciences.

I also want to thank the government of Botswana, whose officials have made a major contribution to the success of the !Kung research. The people of Botswana have been unfailingly courteous and have made us feel welcome time and time again. I hope that this study, and others like it, will repay in a small way the many debts owed to them. A portion of the proceeds from this book is earmarked for the Kalahari Peoples Fund, a nonprofit foundation supporting development projects in Botswana.

Thanks are also due to the members of the Kalahari Research Group for valuable suggestions and criticisms, and for many good times over the years. Though not all of us agree on all issues, I continue to respect their individual and collective views.

For help in reading portions of the manuscript, I want to thank Megan Biesele, Harriet Rosenberg, Jane Schneider, Marjorie Shostak, David Turner, and Annette Weiner—critics who are in no way responsible for any errors this book may contain. Kate Hamilton typed the manuscript with dispatch and élan. A special vote of thanks goes to Harriet Rosenberg, whose dry humor and emotional support sustained me more than she knows.

Finaly, my deepest debt is to the !Kung people of Botswana.

i !ha weyshi //kau ge: May you live in health and peace always.

Contents

A note on the !Kung language

The San languages are characterized by unusual sounds called clicks. These are produced when the tongue is drawn sharply away from various points of articulation on the roof of the mouth. The four clicks used in !Kung appear as follows:

/   Dental click, as in /Xai/xai, /Du/da (in spoken English this sound denotes a mild reproach, written "tsk, tsk").

≠   Alveolar click, as in ≠Toma.

!   Alveopalatal click as in !Kung, n!ore.

//   Lateral click, as in //gangwa (in spoken English this sound is used in some dialects to urge on a horse).

Other features of the San orthography that should be noted include:

~   Nasalization as in /twã.

"   Glottal flap as in //"xa (mongongo) or K"au.

For the nonlinguist, San words may be pronounced by simply dropping the click. For example, for //gangwa read gangwa, and for ≠Toma//gwe read Toma gwe. Dobe rhymes with Toby.

!Kung at the mouth of /Twihaba caves.

1 / The !Kung

These Bushmen are perhaps the same known to the lake people by the name of Makowkow, who live north west of the Batoana, a very independent race [who] possess no cattle . . . a noble independent race of Bushmen [live] at Rietfontein beholden to no one.

Thomas Chapman (1868)

Not far from the border of South West Africa . . . is a group of caves . . . visited by few white people. The journey involves a long and arduous trek across sandy country through which no road passes and a competent guide is essential. . . . The country in the vicinity of these caves is probably the least known in the whole Protectorate and Bushmen and the wild animals have it to themselves.

Anthony Sillery (1952)

Chapman in the 1860s and Sillery almost a century later were referring to the same fabled people—the !Kung San of the Kalahari Desert, fierce and independent, unknown to the outside world until recently. And I was going out to find them. The !Kung, or Zhu/wasi as they call themselves, were virtually unknown to scientists until the 1950s, and now, in October 1963, I was on my way to !Goshe, a waterhole in northwestern Bechuanaland, to make a year-long study of them.

I had traveled a long way from North America, by plane from Berkeley, California, to my home in Toronto; from there to Nairobi, Kenya, where I met my friends and collaborators Irven and Nancy DeVore and their family. We then traveled by Land Rover over half the African continent, arriving in Botswana in August. Irven DeVore and I surveyed the northwestern Kalahari for two weeks looking for a suitable study site, without success. Then, after the DeVores had returned to Harvard, I came back to the Kalahari with two Land Rovers and two African assistants, determined to find the elusive !Kung. The area west of !Goshe appeared to offer our last hope for success.

Hour after hour, our Land Rover ground slowly in four-wheel drive through the deep sand. On the threshold of a great adventure, I retraced in my mind the steps that had brought me to this place. In the early 1960s there had been a renaissance in evolutionary studies in anthropology. Fueled by the Leakeys' fossil discoveries in

1

East Africa, by new dating techniques, by archeological finds and nonhuman primate field research, and by the rediscovery of long-disregarded nineteenth-century classics in evolutionary social anthropology, there was a new and growing interest in studies of the evolution of human behavior. I was part of the generation of anthropology graduate students who were excited by the prospects of a new interdisciplinary synthesis in anthropology, a new view of humanity's beginnings based on the firm data of archeology, physical anthropology, and ethnography.

What particular circumstances had brought me to the Kalahari? The piece of research that had captured *my* imagination was the study of contemporary hunting and gathering peoples. Today few people still live this way, but 12,000 years ago, foraging for wild game and plant foods had been the universal mode of human subsistence. (The term *foragers* or *foraging peoples* is a convenient shorthand for groups with this kind of adaptation.) Our ancestors evolved as foragers, and all basic human institutions—language, marriage, kinship, family, exchange, and human nature itself—were formed during the two- to four-million-year period when we lived by hunting and gathering. Thus the study of the surviving foragers—the San, Inuit (Eskimo), Australian aborigines, and others—had much to teach us.

But in order to be able to learn their lessons we have to exercise the utmost caution. In dealing with a people as exotic as the !Kung, we have to be careful to avoid the twin pitfalls of racism and romanticism. First, foragers like the !Kung are not "missing links"; they are as human as we are, and their histories are as long

On the road to the Dobe area.

as the histories of any other human group. And second, nowhere will we find foragers today living in Pleistocene conditions, that is, as hunters living in a world of hunters. All foragers have been in some contact with nonforaging peoples, some for a very long time. There are no "lost" continents or lost tribes (Wolf 1982), and even the !Kung whom I was on my way to visit had been known to exist and had been named in the nineteenth century.

If one takes these pitfalls carefully into account, there is still much to be learned from contemporary foragers. In fact, it is their very humanity that has made people like the !Kung and other foragers so important for science. These peoples, despite their cultural and geographic diversity, have a core of features in common, and this core of features represents the basic human adaptation stripped of the acretions and complications brought about by agriculture, urbanization, advanced technology, and national and class conflict—all of the "advances" of the last few thousand years.

How do they make a living? How do they organize their communities? How are they able to settle conflicts in the absence of chiefs? These central questions could be studied directly if—and it is a big if—I could find the right people—leading independent lives, getting their own food, and settling their own quarrels. In the 1860s all interior !Kung had lived this way. Even by the 1950s there were still many who did. But this was 1963, and the winds of change were sweeping Africa. Could such an adaptation survive in the jet age?

After many hours of driving we suddenly came upon signs of human settlement, and at sundown we pulled into !Goshe, a row of mud huts that stretched for a mile along a sand ridge. A dozen men, women, and children came out to greet us. The San people of !Goshe were friendly and open. I stammered a few words of greeting in !Kung and passed out tobacco, which they eagerly accepted. However, as I soon learned, most of the !Goshe !Kung worked for their Bantu-speaking neighbors, herding their goats and cattle. They dined on milk and meat, and politically they were subject to their overlords, the aristocratic Tswana. Were there any waterholes, I asked, where !Kung people lived without Blacks and cattle? There was one, they told me, about a full day's travel to the west at a place called Dobe, near the beacon that marked the border with South West Africa. My assistants, Enoch Tabiso and Onesimus Mbombo, and I decided to go to Dobe first thing the next morning.

A WATERHOLE CALLED DOBE

October is the hottest month of the Kalahari year, and by nine a.m. the sun was already a hot disc high in the sky as we drove our Land Rover into the dry pan of Dobe, cut the engine, and waited in the pool of shade of the truck. After ten minutes a cluster of brown figures dressed in leather appeared 100 yards away and stopped in the shade at the pan's edge, waiting silently. We approached them, and I warily sized them up. They were all short, the men about five foot two, the women well under five feet. Their brown skins were deeply seamed with lines from exposure to the sun. They were dressed in sueded leather, the men in tight-fitting breechclouts, the women in beaded aprons and soft skins. Both sexes were naked above the

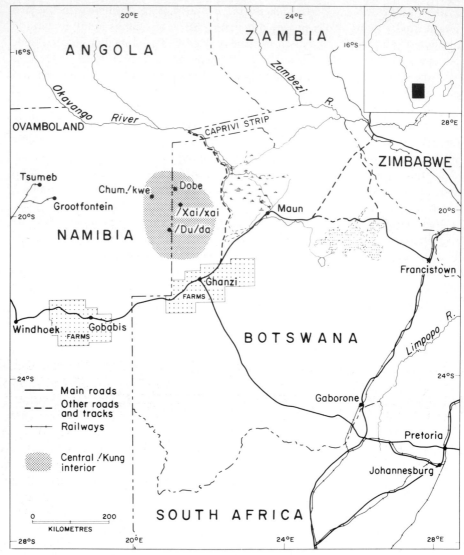

Figure 1–1. The Dobe area in southern Africa.

waist. The women were handsomely adorned with necklaces, arm bands, and hair ornaments of beads made from ostrich eggshells. Both sexes wore their densely curled hair close cropped, and as I observed them more closely I saw that their high foreheads and cheekbones were etched with geometric lines of tattooing that showed up blue under their golden skins. Each of the men wore a bow and quiver in a sling over his shoulder, and two of them had spears in their hands, but on the whole they seemed friendly enough. After a few minutes, Onesimus broke the silence with greetings in Tswana. Then, in my one sentence of !Kung, I asked "*a !ku re o a zhuwe?*" (What is your name?) of each in turn.

"*Mi o ≠Toma*," responded the first, a small, wizened man in his sixties with a sardine can key hanging from his ear.

"*Mi o ≠Toma*," said a handsome young man in his thirties wearing a shredded western cloth cap.

"*Mi o N!eishi*," replied a barrel-chested man in his late fifties whose deep-set eyes smiled in a sea of wrinkles.

"*Mi o Tin!ay*," a handsome middle-aged woman with full lips spoke next.

"*Mi o //Koka*," said a very old and spry woman in a leather *kaross* that seemed too big for her.

"*Mi o //Gumin!a*," said a tiny, dignified old woman with a twinkle in her eye.

Finally a young woman with a baby at her breast and a four-year-old at her side said, "*Mi n/a o Sa//gai*."

The nine people who came out to meet us were core members of the Dobe camp, a strongly independent group of people who, we later learned, had been associated with the waterhole for over thirty years and who preferred to live on their own in the "bush" rather than share a waterhole with cattle and goats.

They were related to one another as follows (Figure 1–2).

//Koka and her younger brother N!eishi were core "owners" of Dobe along with their spouses—the formidable old ≠Toma //gwe (≠Toma sourplum) and

≠Toma//gwe and the men of Dobe.

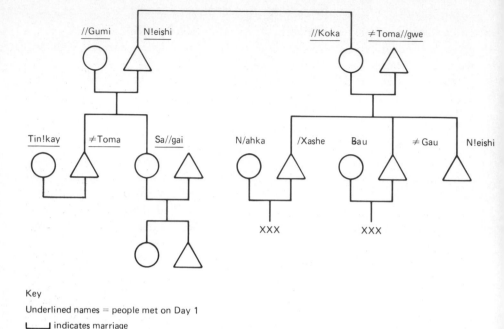

Key

Underlined names = people met on Day 1

⌐ ⌐ indicates marriage

⌐ ⌐ indicates siblingship

△   male

○   female

Figure 1–2. The Core of the Dobe Camp.

the diminutive //Gumin!a (Old //Gumi). ≠Toma//gwe and //Koka had three married sons in their thirties who were away hunting with their wives and children, while //Gumi and N!eishi had a married son and a married daughter—the younger ≠Toma and Sa//gai who were present to greet us.

I asked them if I could come and stay with them and learn !Kung, and after much discussion they agreed. Would they be interested in learning English in return? This question, when it passed through the interpreters, was greeted with gales of laughter. ≠Toma //gwe chortled no, that the sounds the Europeans made were much too difficult for him. I replied that *we* found their click sounds impossible to pronounce. This was met with puzzled but sympathetic looks. Imagine anyone finding clicks difficult, they seemed to be saying!

As the tension eased //Gumin!a asked for *shoro,* the !Kung word for tobacco, and the others joined in. When we gave them some of the strong leaf tobacco they favored they pulled out what appeared to be Western-style commercial briar pipes, which they lit with flint and steel kits. The pipes, in fact, turned out to be home-made replicas of our pipes, complete to the last detail, including a contrasting mouthpiece carved in black wood.

As the odor of strong tobacco swirled around us, we talked and talked—of where I was to camp, where to draw water, where the wild foods were—and passed pipes-ful of tobacco around at frequent intervals as the sun rose in the sky. Finally, when

//Koka cooking meat.

the details were settled and we were about to disperse, ≠Toma //gwe indicated to the interpreter that he had one more thing to say.

"Some years ago," he began in a voice that was both warm and scolding, "a man called Mashalo, his wife Norna, and his children came to live at a place called /Gausha to the west.[1] Many good things happened," he continued, "to the people of /Gausha as a result of Mashalo being there: blankets, clothes, pots, knives, beads all came their way. But none of this good fortune reached us in Dobe. We were sad and just lived. Now that you have come, our hearts are glad. Now we have a White man of our own. We waited so long. It's about time that you've come. We expect good things from you, so don't disappoint us. And another thing," his voice was rising in pitch, "if you have anything to give away, give everything to us, not to those other people." His hand gesture indicated points east, west, and south, covering most of the known !Kung villages.

I was floored by this last speech. With extraordinary aplomb, the old man had managed to welcome me, while criticizing me for not coming sooner, and admonish *me* to be generous while baldly stating that *he* for his part was going to keep everything for himself!

Stunned, I got back into the truck and headed off to pitch camp. Clearly this fieldwork was not going to be a piece of cake. The people were friendly, but not pushovers, and they seemed to have at least some of the personality quirks that afflicted people in urban society. ≠Toma certainly lived up to his nickname: the sour plum. Yet there was something likable about ≠Toma's frankness. I thought to myself, I'm going to like it here.

In the evening I reflected on the day's events. So these were the !Kung of fable and legend. Now, brought face to face with an all-too-human reality, it was a conscious effort for me to conjure up the grand theories of human evolution that had set my odyssey in motion. The Dobe !Kung seemed so familiar. ≠Toma//gwe, with his sardine-key earring, infectious laugh, and rudeness, reminded me of a

---

[1] A reference to the family of Laurence and Lorna Marshall who had conducted fieldwork at Nyae Nyae in the 1950s.

Sal//gai and her son ≠Toma.

crochetty great-uncle of mine back in Toronto;   and N!eishi with the broad shoulders and deep chest reminded me of my own father (much later, in fact, N!eishi adopted me as his son).

It became clear that an enormous task lay before me—to make sense of the thriving contemporary !Kung culture with all its complexities and contradictions. I had to count the people, learn their language, find out what they ate and what ate them (both physically and spiritually), and make sense, if possible, of the paradoxes of generosity and selfishness that seemed to lurk beneath the surface of their lives. The building of evolutionary theories would have to wait for the time being, on the back burner.

I was to spend the better part of the next ten years trying to unravel these and other paradoxes the !Kung presented. But for the moment I turned to the immediate task of pitching a tent to protect us from the onrushing heat of the October Kalahari.

2/The people of the Dobe area

When Dutch explorers reached the Cape of Good Hope in the seventeenth century, they found two kinds of people living there. First were the numerous cattle- and goat-herding peoples, whom the Dutch named the *Hottentots*, a term that mimics their strange (to the Dutch) click-filled language. These people called themselves *Khoi* ("people"), the term they are known by today. Second were the nonherding peoples, similar in language and appearance to the Khoi, but who kept no livestock, living on wild plants, animals, and shellfish. The Khoi called them *Sonqua,* or *San,* a Khoi term that means "aborigines" or "settlers proper." Because they were elusive and shy and lived in much smaller groups than the Khoi, the Dutch named them *Bojesmans,* that is, people of the bush—*Bushmen*—a term by which they were known until recently to the rest of the world. Although widely used, the term *Bushman* has both racist and sexist connotations. Recognizing these problems, many researchers have agreed to call them the *San,* and I would urge my readers to do the same.

For thousands of years the Khoi and the San occupied most of southern Africa west of the Bantu-speaking peoples in the Eastern Cape. But as White settlement expanded north in the eighteenth century, bitter conflicts arose with the native peoples, conflicts that escalated into genocidal warfare against the San. By the late nineteenth century the San had been virtually exterminated within the boundaries of the present-day Republic of South Africa, and most writers of the day spoke of them as a dying race. As exploration pushed farther north, however, the grim obituary on the San proved, happily, to be premature. In the security of the Kalahari Desert, thousands of San continued to live as hunter-gatherers in relatively peaceful proximity to a variety of neighboring Black herders and farmers. By the mid-1950s, physical anthropologists, linguists, and archeologists had begun to map out the numbers and distribution of the living San. They are now estimated to number close to 50,000, a figure that appears to be on the increase (Table 2–1, Figure 2–1).

WHO ARE THE SAN?

The San are a cluster of indigenous peoples in Southern Africa who speak a click language and who have a tradition of living by hunting and gathering. They are to be distinguished from the Khoi, whom they resemble physically, by the Khoi's

TABLE 2–1   ESTIMATED NUMBERS OF CONTEMPORARY SAN.

Language Group[2]	Botswana	Namibia	Angola	Other	Total
1. Tshu-Khwe	22,000	4,500	500	500	27,500
2. Southern !Xo, etc.	2,500	500	[1]	[1]	3,000
3. Northern !Kung, etc.	4,500	12,000	3,000	[1]	19,500
	29,000	17,000	3,500	500	50,000

[1] Less than 100.
[2] A fourth language group—//Xam—is now virtually extinct in South Africa, though some Botswana populations may be related to it.

possession of livestock, and from the Bantu by marked physical, linguistic, and cultural differences.

San come in a variety of shapes and sizes. Many are short and pale-skinned, while others are tall and dark-skinned like their Bantu-speaking neighbors. This variability has prompted a rough division of the San on physical grounds into the "Yellow" and "Black" San.

The Black San include peoples in southeastern Angola, western Zambia, and eastern Botswana who speak languages of the *Tshu-Khwe* group and whose economy is based on mixed herding, farming, foraging, and wage labor. It also includes the Nama- and !Kung-speaking Heillom in northern Namibia. The Black San are genetically indistinguishable from surrounding Bantu populations, and it is likely that their gene pools have been augmented by the influx of Bantu-speaking refugees from the colonial wars and raiding of the nineteenth century.

The "Yellow" San are found in southern Angola, western and central Botswana, and northern and eastern Namibia. They speak languages of three different language families: the Northern !Kung, the Central Tshu-Khwe, and the Southern. !Xo, (A fourth language family—the //Xam—is virtually extinct in South Africa). Linguistically diverse, they are physically similar to one another: short, pale-skinned, deep-chested, with straight foreheads and small, almost delicate faces and jaws. The latter are the distinctive features of *neotony*—the retention of infantile traits into adult life—a trend that is found to some extent in all modern populations of *Homo sapiens*. Economically, the "Yellow" San include full-time gatherer-hunters (increasingly rare), mixed farmers and herders, and since the 1960s, a growing number of farm and migrant laborers.

The numbers and distribution of the contemporary San are shown in Table 2–1.

STUDIES OF THE SAN

Modern *ethnographic* studies of the San begin with the expeditions of Laurence and Lorna Marshall and their family to the !Kung of Nyae Nyae in 1951. Their many fields trips since 1952 have produced a distinguished series of books (see L. Marshall 1976, and E. M. Thomas 1959) and films by John Marshall (see film guide, pp. 161–164). The more southerly /Gwi San of the Central Kalahari have

Figure 2–1. The Distribution of the San in Africa.

been studied by Silberbauer (1965, 1981), Tanaka (1980), and Cashdan (1981), while the southernmost of the contemporary San, the !Xo, have been studied by Heinz (1966, 1972), Eibl-Eibesfeldt (1972), and Sbrzesny (1976). The Naron (Nharo), a sedentary group living on farms and cattle posts, have been studied by Bleek (1928), Guenther (1970), and Barnard (1976). Research on !Xo linguistics has been done by Traill (1974). Vierich (1982) and Hitchcock (1982) have done detailed studies of San economic change in the eastern Kalahari.

The most extensively studied San group has been the !Kung San of the Dobe area. Starting out in 1963 with a two-person team consisting of Irven DeVore and myself, the Kalahari Research Project has grown to include a dozen specialists in many fields.[1]

Today the Dobe !Kung are probably the world's best-documented foraging society. There have been book-length studies published on ecology and society by Lee (1979), on ethnoarcheology (Yellen 1977), on demography (Howell 1979), and on healing (Katz 1982). Shostak has published a superb autobiography of Nisa, a Dobe !Kung woman (1981, 1983). Studies of all these subjects, plus genetics, health, folklore, child rearing, and other topics, have been published in a collection of papers edited by Lee and DeVore (1976). More recently, Dobe !Kung economic and exchange systems have been studied by Wiessner (1977, 1982), and their nutrition, physiology, and cultural history have been studied by Wilmsen (1978, 1981).

Although this book is based largely on my own field research, I will frequently draw on the published research of these other specialists.

THE DOBE AREA

What sort of a place is the Dobe area, scene of so many studies of !Kung life? It consists of a cluster of ten waterholes north and south of the Aha Hills in the northwest Kalahari desert. The area can be conveniently divided into three divisions. The more northern waterholes are strung out along the length of the !Kangwa Molapo, a 100-kilometer-long dry river valley that has its source in the Nyae Nyae area of Namibia and wends its way eastward through Botswana before disappearing in the desert west of the Okavango Swamps. Unlike the rest of the sandy Kalahari, the !Kangwa Molapo traverses an area of limestone and granite outcrops. The !Kung name for the area, N/umsi, meaning "the region of rocks or stones," reflects this geological oddity. In addition to the permanent waterpoints, the !Kangwa valley has a hinterland of gathering and hunting areas to the north, east, and west of about 3000 square kilometers.

South of the Ahas a smaller dry river valley, the /Xai/xai Molapo, forms the main axis of settlement, with its one major waterhole at /Xai/xai Pan and a hinterland containing many smaller seasonal waterpoints to the west, south, and east.

In the center are the Aha Hills themselves, consisting of several scattered ranges of low hills 100 meters above the surrounding plain.

About 70 percent of the !Kung live in N!umsi, while the remainder live at /Xai/xai. The Aha Hills, because of lack of surface water, contain no permanent settlements. About one-third of the Dobe area lies across the border in Namibia. Since the building of a border fence by South Africa in 1965 this western portion of the area has been cut off to gathering and hunting !Kung.

---

[1] Members of the original Kalahari Research group included: Megan Biesele, Nicholas Blurton-Jones, Irven DeVore, Nancy DeVore, Patricia Draper, John Hansen, Henry Harpending, Nancy Howell, Richard Katz, Melvin Konner, Richard Lee, Marjorie Shostak, Stewart Truswell, and John Yellen.

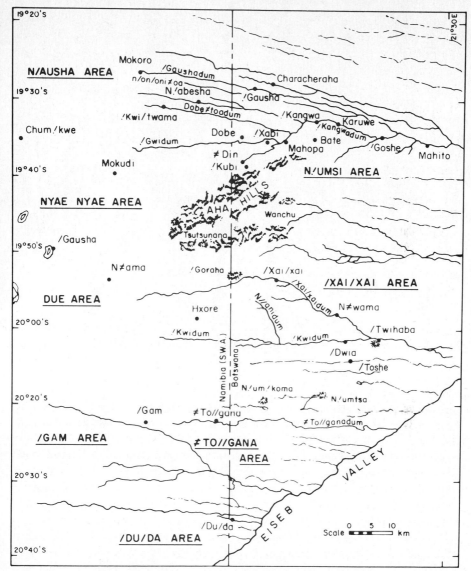

Figure 2–2. The Dobe area and surrounding regions.

Together, the three regions of the Dobe area in both Botswana and Namibia comprise an area of about 8000 square kilometers (3000 square miles). The area's features and its waterholes are shown in Figure 2–2.

EXPLORING THE DOBE AREA

After my initial contacts with ≠Toma //gwe and his kin, I built a camp at Dobe. The !Kung suggested several spots that didn't appeal to me, and so I picked a

Lee exploring the Dobe area on donkeyback.

pleasant grove of trees on the edge of a stony pan. All was well until the first rains came. We woke up one morning ankle-deep in water, with the !Kung standing at the door of my tent laughing until the tears came to their eyes.

Packing quickly, we moved our camp with its sodden bedding to a better-drained location, and I proceeded with my work. The first order of business was to get a sense of the immediate area. On foot, by truck, and, later on, donkeyback, I spent the better part of two months visiting each waterhole in turn, counting the people and getting a sense of the economic basis of each locale.

The !Kung population in 1964 stood at 466, with 379 residents and 87 seasonal visitors. There were also some 340 Blacks with their cattle resident in the area (Table 2–2). Although !Kung occupied all the waterholes, each grouping had its own distinctive features.

!Goshe was the easternmost settlement in the area. With a population of 75 !Kung and 30 Blacks, !Goshe was also the most acculturated of all the !Kung settlements. The !Kung had lived with and worked for the Blacks for decades, herding their cattle and tending their fields. Some !Goshe families had acquired herds of their own, and a substantial portion of their diet now consists of milk, meat, eggs, and grains. When I arrived they were already relatively sedentary, having occupied the same villages for over five years. Their relative wealth set !Goshe people somewhat apart from other !Kung. They tended to marry amongst themselves, yet they still participated in reciprocal exchanges with other !Kung who visited them, often giving a bag of grain in exchange for a wild product. Among the !Kung and

TABLE 2-2   POPULATION OF THE DOBE AREA BY WATERHOLE, 1964.

	San & Resident	Marginal	Total	Blacks
!Goshe	75	0	75	30
!Kangwa Matse	9	0	9	–
!Kangwa	36	0	36	72
Bate	41	3	44	29
Mahopa	33	10	43	65
!Xabi	10	0	10	12
!Kubi	23	25	48	65
/Xai/xai	117	30	147	67
Dobe	35	0	35	0
Other	0	19	19	0
	379	87	466	340

Blacks alike, !Goshe was famous as a center of ritual and medicine. Healing dances were held frequently (almost daily at times), and a !Goshe woman named /Twan!a pioneered the introduction of the important woman's healing dance—!Gwahtsi (see Chapter 8).

Traveling west up the !Kangwa Valley for 11 kilometers (7 miles) one arrived at the waterhole of !Kangwa Matse—small !Kangwa. With a population of nine !Kung and a few Blacks, it was little more than a cattle-post suburb of !Kangwa.

Five kilometers farther to the west was !Kangwa, the major settlement in the !Kangwa valley. The community takes its name from the !Kangwa Rock Spring, an abundant and perennial source of clear, cool water. !Kangwa was the administrative center or kgotla of the District, the headquarters of the Tribal Headman and the Tax Collector. At !Kangwa the 72 Blacks outnumbered San, and the !Kung population of 36 subsisted by a combination of working for the Tswana headman, herding the Blacks' cattle, and gathering and hunting.

Eight kilometers south of !Kangwa, at the base of the Aha mountains, were the Bate villages, home of 41 !Kung and 29 Blacks. The !Kung kinship links were to !Kangwa and Mahopa, and many relatives liked to visit Bate in the fall to eat the delicious Marula nuts for which Bate was famous.

Three separate waterpoints constituted the Mahopa waterhole, strung out in the bed of the !Kangwa River. With a population of 65 Blacks and 2000 cattle, Mahopa was a major center for !Kung employment as herders for the Blacks. The 33 Mahopa !Kung had close ties to Bate, !Kangwa, and Dobe, and the camps saw a constant stream of visitors from west and east. Subsistence was based on about 75 percent gathered and hunted foods and about 25 percent grains and milk. Mahopa people also had attempted to plan their own crops, with varying degrees of success.

A crossroads, !Xabi was a small waterhole three miles east of Dobe, occupied principally by the family of the Tswana Headman, his Herero wife, and his !Kung clients: population 10 !Kung, 12 Blacks.

South of !Xabi was !Kubi, a populous waterhole in the forests at the base of the Aha Hills. The population of 65 Herero provided employment for the 23 !Kung residents. These Herero arrived after 1954 as a result of a major shift of population in the western fringes of the Okavango swamps. !Kubi, it turned out, has been the

The main Dobe camp, spring 1964.

site of hunter-gatherer life for tens of thousands of years. The Middle Stone Age prehistoric site of ≠Gi, excavated by John Yellen and Alison Brooks, lies only a kilometer from !Kubi Pan (Brooks and Yellen 1979). In the early 1960s the !Kubi !Kung maintained close ties with the !Kung of Nyae Nyae and had extensively intermarried with them. The !Kubi waterhole was also famous locally for its Marula nuts, and it was and is the only source of Baobab fruit and Tsin beans in the northern Dobe area.

The most exotic and interesting of all the waterholes for me was /Xai/xai, which lay 28 kilometers (17 miles) south of !Kubi across the Aha Hills. The 117 !Kung and 67 Blacks were dispersed in ten villages around the perimeter of the /Xai/xai pan. Each of these villages had access to a hinterland for gathering and hunting. In general, villages on the east side of /Xai/xai pan gathered to the east, villages on the north side had a northern hinterland, and so on. Not far from /Xai/xai to the east were the legendary caves of /Twihaba, one of the geological wonders of Botswana that Sillery spoke about with such awe (see Chapter 1).

/Xai/xai had been a meeting place for well over a century, and probably longer. Bands from the four corners of the !Kung world traditionally gathered there in the dry season to trade, dance, and arrange marriages. Today this history is reflected in the far-reaching ties that /Xai/xai !Kung maintain with !Kung to the north, west, south, and east. Later in my stay with the !Kung I was to live at /Xai/xai for fourteen months.

My tour of the area brought me back to Dobe, my spiritual home for the first fifteen months of my fieldwork. I named the region the Dobe area in honor of my adopted waterhole. A small, inaccessible spring deep in a rock cleft provided the sole source of water for the 35 !Kung of Dobe, the one waterhole in the 1960s with no non-!Kung or livestock resident. Centered around the families of 70-year-old //Kokan/a and her younger brother N!eishi, the Dobe camps consisted largely of more conservative !Kung who preferred to live on their own rather than herd cattle for Blacks. They remained on good terms with Blacks at Mahopa, where they frequently visited to ask for some milk, the staple of the Herero diet. These handouts supplemented a diet that, during the 1960s, varied from 85 to 100 percent gathered-and-hunted foods. Vast mongongo forests lie within a day's walk north and west of Dobe (see Chapter 4).

A HISTORY OF CONTACT

As my work continued, I began to get a sense of the recent history of the Dobe area. Later, archeologists added information on a much deeper time scale. An exciting picture began to emerge.

From the archeological record, the Dobe area has been a hunting and gathering stronghold for literally thousands of years. Middle Stone Age materials dating to 20,000 B.C. have been found at ≠Gi and elsewhere. We have no way of knowing when the ancestors of the contemporary !Kung first arrived. but judging from the unbroken deposits of Later Stone Age materials underlying contemporary !Kung villages, it was at least a thousand years ago, and probably several thousand. The Dobe !Kung themselves have no tradition of being refugees from other areas.

Trading contacts with Bantu-speaking peoples to the east and north were established as early as several hundred years ago (Wilmsen 1981), but no permanent *settlement* of the interior by non-!Kung is evident before the twentieth century.

The first contacts that can be adequately documented date from the period 1870–1920. As recently as a little over a century ago, ancestral bands of !Kung San roamed the interior of what is now the Dobe area still hunting with bone arrows. Iron arrowheads only came into general use during the lifetimes of the grandparents of my oldest informants. The first non-San to penetrate the area (in modern times) were Tswana herders from the east. From the 1870s on they came during the summer rains to trade, hunt, and graze their cattle. After some initial shyness, the !Kung were quickly incorporated into the Tswana tributary system. The !Kung acted as trackers for the Tswana and helped butcher the meat, and when the summer had passed they acted as porters, carrying the season's take of their new overlords back to the east. A !Kung man describes this period:

> The type of work that we !Kung entered then was called *n/i //wana !ha* ["shoulder the meat-carrying yoke"]. The country was teeming with game, and the Tswanas came up on horseback with guns. They put us under the carrying yoke. We had to carry the meat that they shot from the kill sites back to the camps; and then at the end of the summer hunting season, a line of porters would carry bales of *biltong* [dried meat strips] back to Tsau. Then there they would be paid off in balls of *shoro* [tobacco], which they carried back to the West. We !Kung also did our own hunting, and brought the hides and *biltong* in for tobacco.

From the late 1870s, European hunters from the south also came to the Dobe area to seek the rich resources of ivory, rhino horn, and fur-bearing animals. Some men had affairs with !Kung women, and the descendents of these unions today live at !Kubi. (It was not until the 1950s that the first Europeans lived for any length of time in the interior.) In !Kung oral history the period 1870–1920 is sometimes called the time of *Koloi* (Tswana-wagons), a reference to the oxwagons that the Tswana later brought with them on their annual trips.

The largest number of non-!Kung in the Dobe area are members of the Herero people. The Herero are southwestern Bantu-speakers who have a long history in the territory of Namibia. During the tragic war of 1904–1907 thousands of Herero were slaughtered by the Germans. Several thousand Herero escaped across the desert and were given asylum in the then-British colony of Bechuanaland (Botswana). After 1920 the ruling Tswana gave a few families of Herero permission to settle in the Dobe area, and this event marked the beginning of a new era for the Dobe !Kung. These contacts are discussed in Chapter 9.

European presence in the Dobe area occurred at an even later date. The first government patrol to reach Dobe from Bechuanaland dates from 1934. The area really became known to outsiders when the Marshall family began their studies of the adjacent Nyae Nyae area in 1951. Even after the Nyae Nyae !Kung had been settled on a government station at Chum!kwe in 1960, the Dobe people continued to live in relative isolation. During my first year in the field only about one truck every six weeks reached the Dobe area. Although the !Kung of Dobe had seen many Whites, I was the first to live in their area, and this fact created a certain bond between us.[2] The major changes that occurred after 1970, after my main fieldwork was completed, are detailed in Chapter 10.

[2] Strictly speaking, I was not the first White. A man named Venter (called Fendare by the !Kung) lived with his Nama wife at !Kubi for some years after 1927. Also, although a number of anthropologists worked in the Dobe area after 1964, for the first year I was there on my own. Irven and Nancy DeVore rejoined me at Dobe only after October 1964.

3 / Environment and settlement

The Dobe area quickly began to captivate my senses. The October days were fiercely hot and drowsy, with the smells of countless aromatic shrubs and trees hanging heavily in the air. Bird calls were a constant background to the day's activities. There were the staccato rhythms of the woodpeckers, the cooing of the turtle doves, the sharp, high-pitched cries of the plovers, and the characteristic *kooweeei* of the grey loerie that the local English called the go-away bird. The giant dung beetles and other exotic insects went about their daily business. Swarms of stingless bees hovered about the waterhole. Wildlife was abundant. Antelope and warthog tracks were everywhere, as well as leopard and hyena. At night lions could be heard grunting to each other as they fed on their kills.

At midday the land was a furnace. Since walking in the sun could consume a quart of body water per hour through sweat, during the hottest part of the day the people rested. At dusk the burning heat broke its grip on the land and life became animated. Firewood was gathered, nuts were roasted, and food was cooked in iron pots. As night fell the firelight rose in intensity to cast an orange glow over people, dogs, huts, and trees.

But my favorite time was after dark. In the cool I could sit in front of my tent on a canvas folding chair and observe the heavens. On moonlit nights the light was incredibly bright, light enough to read by. And when the moon set I saw a heavenly display the likes of which I didn't know existed. The sky became a dense mass of points of light. Literally thousands of stars were visible, not the paltry few hundred that the reflected city lights allow us in the northern sky. The !Kung call the Milky Way *!gu !ko!kemi*, "the backbone of the sky," and the ridge of stars overhead with dozens of patches of interstellar dust does look like a vertebral column.

The habitat intrigued me. I resolved to learn as much about it as I could, and wherever I went in those first few months I was constantly peppering the !Kung with questions. "What kind of plant is this? What soil does it grow on? Do you eat it? What animals eat it? Does it have any use to you?" The !Kung enjoyed this kind of work. They were superb botanists and could read the landscape like a road map. Daily my knowledge of the environment grew.

The Dobe area is part of a vast basin 1000 to 1200 meters above sea level, bisected by the Botswana-Namibia border on the northern fringe of the Kalahari Desert. The first impression of a traveler to this region is an immense flatness, where the sky dominates the landscape. The Aha Hills rise only 100 meters above the

19

surrounding plain, and from their top one sees what seem to be endless vistas of brush and savannah stretching to the horizon in every direction. Thus the observer is surprised to find in the !Kung language of travel a rich vocabulary of climbing and descending as they discuss trips from one waterhole to another. For example, a trip to Nokaneng is always referred to as *kowa //hai* (literally, "to descend to the east"). As one gains familiarity with the area, one realizes that the !Kung are right: there are slight elevation differences from place to place, and I soon came to appreciate how important these differences are in the structuring of drainage, vegetation zones, and key plant resources.

At several points in the landscape the sandy plain is broken by dry river courses like the !Kangwa and the /Xai/xai. Some of these river courses can be traced for 100 kilometers. They rarely hold flowing water, perhaps twice in a decade, but when they do the flow of water can be considerable. In a few localities the underlying rock formations are exposed. These rocks form an important source of subsurface water. Some areas are riddled with sinkholes and caves, such as the extensive underground network of caves at /Twihaba (known as Drodsky's Caves), which are mentioned in Chapter 1.

The upper reaches of the !Kangwa Valley are extremely flat. When one reaches !Kangwa, however, the relief becomes much sharper. By !Goshe the riverbed is a 7 meter-deep miniature canyon between vertical banks. Here the down-cutting of the river has exposed deposits of high-quality chert, a rich source of prehistoric tools, and, today, of flints for the flint-and-steel fire-making kits used by the !Kung. In fact, the lower !Kangwa descends so steeply that after a heavy rainfall the river bed becomes a raging torrent for a few hours, with cascades to challenge a whitewater canoeist.

THE DUNE AND *MOLAPO* SYSTEM

Apart from hills and dry rivers, the main feature of the Dobe area is a system of fixed longitudinal dunes running parallel to each other and oriented roughly east-west. The dune crests and flanks have deep, loose red and white sands. The *molapos* (river courses, in Setswana) between the dunes and in the more deeply incised river valleys, are characterized by compacted, fine-grained gray soils. Each supports a distinctive association of trees and shrubs with a distinctive array of edible species.

The !Kung themselves distinguish four kinds of habitats: (1) dunes, (2) flats, (3) *molapos*, and (4) hardpan and river valleys.

Dunes   Unlike the moving dunes of the Namib and Southern Kalahari deserts, the dunes of the Northern Kalahari are fixed by vegetation. *Ricinodendron rautanenii* (the mongongo nut), the major plant food of the Dobe-area !Kung, is found only on the crests of the fixed dunes. The mongongo provides a protein-rich nut meat and a nutritious fruit, and the tree's hollow interior traps rainwater for drinking.

Flats   Intermediate in elevation between the dunes and the *molapos* are plains of buff-to-white compacted sands. The flats provide extensive groves of *Grewia* berry bushes, the vegetable ivory palm with its tasty fruit, and a number of other edible species.

!Kangwa spring in the dry season.

The same view during a heavy rainy season.

Molapos   Two subtypes can be distinguished here. The smaller *molapos* have compacted soils of light gray or buff. Here are found dense thickets of small trees verging on forests. Well-defined *molapos*, with gray, compacted, silty soils and occasional beds of hardpan, support many species of *Acacia* with their edible gums.

Hardpan   The soils here consist of patches of bare rock alternating with patches of sand or mud. The baobab tree with its fruit and seed is the most important food found here.

Water Sources

The northern Kalahari is a semidesert, and water scarcity is a major problem. The !Kung rely on a hierarchy of water sources ranked in order of abundance. First are the permanent waterholes found in the main river bottoms where the bedrock is exposed. Most of these waterholes are natural, but all have been improved and maintained either by the San themselves or, more recently, by the Blacks. Second are the seasonal waters that exist for one to six months a year: these are found in the *molapos* between the dunes, where local drainage patterns produce a depression. These vary from small depressions 15 feet in diameter and ankle-deep, holding water for a few weeks after heavy rains, to great ponds up to 300 feet long, holding water for months or even year-round in years of high rainfall.

Third in importance are the small quantities of water found in the hollow interiors of mongongo and other trees. And finally, there are several species of water-bearing root, which may be dug up and used in emergencies. With these sources

A seasonal pan during the rainy season.

the !Kung plan their annual round, spending the winter season close to the permanent waters and the summer months ranging widely at the secondary and lesser water sources.

FAUNA

Despite recent changes, the Dobe area harbors an impressive array of African plains game. With over 50 resident mammal species, the area can still provide the !Kung with a solid hunting subsistence base. At the same time, the !Kung hunters have to compete for their prey with representatives of all the major predator species: lions, leopards, and others. In addition to the mammals, 90 species of birds, 25 species of reptiles and amphibians, and up to 90 species of invertebrates are also known to the !Kung, making a total of about 260 named species in their animal universe.

Ungulates (hoofed mammals) are the main game animals of the !Kung. Most prominent are kudu, wildebeest, and gemsbok. Giraffe, eland, roan antelope, and hartebeest are also present. The nonmigratory warthog, steenbok, and duiker are extremely plentiful and are the most frequently killed of the ungulates.

Lion, leopard, cheetah, hyena (two species), wild dog, and a dozen smaller forms of carnivores are all found in the Dobe area. Their kills and tracks are frequently encountered on gathering trips, yet the !Kung do not seem to be afraid of them. The !Kung sleep in the open without fires when necessary and make no provision to protect or fortify their living sites.

Of other mammals, the elephant is the only large nonungulate regularly seen in the Dobe area. A few pass through the area each rainy season. In an exceptionally wet year, such as 1973–1974, a dozen might be seen. Buffalo and sometimes hippo are also summer visitors. Of the small- to medium-sized mammals, four are important in the diet: ant bear, porcupine, springhare, and scrub hare. The pangolin (scaly anteater) is less common but is also eaten. Completing the list of mammals are one shrew, two species of squirrel, three species of bat, and 14 species of mouse and gerbil. None of these small mammals are eaten by the !Kung. Finally, there are three primates, also not eaten: the tiny galago, the vervet monkey, and the baboon; the latter two are rarely seen. A summary of the mammals is found in Table 3–1.

Considering the dryness of the area, birdlife is surprisingly abundant. About 100 species of birds are resident in the Dobe area, and another 40 are summer migrants. Of these, the !Kung have identified at least 90 species. The abundant ostrich, though rarely hunted for food, is prized for its eggs. They are emptied, their contents eaten, and the shells cleaned and used for water canteens and in bead making. Other important game birds include the very abundant guinea fowl and francolin, and ducks, korhaan, sandgrouse, quail, and dove.

Twenty-five species of reptiles and amphibians have been recorded, including snakes, lizards, tortoises, chameleons, and frogs. The six kinds of poisonous snakes loom large in the lives of the !Kung. Although snakebites are rare (only three cases occurred in ten years, none fatal), the !Kung take precautions to clear their

TABLE 3–1   MAMMALS OF THE DOBE AREA.

Animal	Occurrence*	Animal	Occurrence
Ungulates		*Other*	
Buffalo	R	Ant bear	C
Duiker	VC	Baboon	VR
Eland	U	Bat (3 species)	C
Gemsbok	C	Elephant	R
Giraffe	U	Galago	C
Hartebeest	U	Scrub hare	VC
Impala	VR	Mouse (12 species)	VC
Kudu	C	Pangolin	C
Roan antelope	U	Porcupine	C
Steenbok	VC	Shrew	C
Warthog	VC	Springhare	VC
Wildebeest	C	Bush squirrel	U
Zebra	R	Ground squirrel	C
		Vervet	R
Carnivores			
Aardwolf	C		
Bat-eared fox	C		
Caracal	U		
Cheetah	C		
Genet	C		
Honey badger	C		
Brown hyena	VR		
Spotted hyena	C		
Black-backed jackal	C		
Leopard	U		
Lion	C		
Banded mongoose	C		
Slender mongoose	C		
Yellow mongoose	C		
Serval	VR		
Wild cat	C		
Wild dog	C		
Zorilla	C		

* VC = very common, daily sights of tracks;
  C = common, weekly sightings of tracks;
  U = uncommon, monthly sightings of tracks;
  R = rare, few sightings per year or less;
  VR = very rare, one or two sightings in a decade.

campsites of brush that would conceal a snake, and whenever they find a poisonous snake, they kill it with a club or digging stick. (Women appear to be as proficient as men at killing snakes.)

Fish are not present in the Dobe area, but aquatic species such as terrapin, leeches, clams, and snails are found in isolated waterholes, indicating a time in the past when the area was connected to a river system by flowing water.

Of the countless invertebrates in the Dobe area, about 85 to 90 species are known to the San, including an abundance of scorpions, spiders, ticks, millipedes, and centipedes, and some 70 species of insects. Few insects are eaten. Wild honey is a superb delicacy but highly subject to seasonal fluctuation. No honey was seen in 1963–1964, but it was fairly common and highly prized in 1967–1969. The most important of the insects for subsistence are the species of *chrysomelid* beetles used by the !Kung for poisoning their hunting arrows. The grubs produce a slow-acting but highly effective poison, which when applied to arrows can kill a wounded animal in 6 to 24 hours.

CLIMATE

With a mean elevation of 1100 meters above sea level, the Dobe area lies within the summer rainfall zone of Southern Africa. The area experiences hot summers with a four-to-six-month rainy season and moderate-to-cool winters without rainfall. The hottest months of the year are October to February, when temperatures average 30 to 40 degrees Centigrade (86 to 104 degrees Fahrenheit). In June and July, the coldest months of the year, night temperatures fall to freezing or near freezing, but they rise during the day to a comfortable 24 to 27 degrees Centigrade (75 to 80 degrees Fahrenheit). Temperatures are fairly consistent from year to year, but this is not the case with rainfall. The annual precipitation may vary from year to year by as much as 500 percent.

The Seasonal Round

The !Kung accurately divide the year into five seasons (Figure 3–1).

!Huma (spring rains) Their year begins with the first rains in October and November. These are light thundershowers that often fall on one area and miss other areas entirely. This is a spectacular area for lightning. According to the United States Weather Service, Botswana has one of the highest incidences of lightning in the world. Brilliant displays light the Dobe sky at this time of year. The first rains also have the effect of triggering growth in plants and reproduction in animals, and overnight the parched landscape is transformed into one of lush greenery.

BARA	≠TOBE	/GUM	/GAʌ	/HUMA
Summer	Autumn	Winter	Early Spring	Spring Rains
HOT RAINY	COOLER DRYING	COOL VERY DRY	HOT DRY	HOT DRY/WET
D J	F M	A M J	J A S	O N

Figure 3–1. Seasons of the !Kung.

Filling ostrich eggshells from a small summer waterhole.

Bara (main summer rains)   From December to March the heaviest rains fall, bringing with them a season of plenty. Migratory ducks, geese, and other waterfowl flock to the seasonal pans in great numbers. Elephant and buffalo may migrate from the Okavango swamps. The major summer plant foods—fruits, berries, melons, and leafy greens—also make their appearance, and the !Kung camps are widely distributed at seasonal waterpoints in the hinterland.

≠Tobe (autumn)   A brief autumn occurs in April or May after the rains have ceased but before the onset of the really cold weather. The seasonal pans shrink and dry out at this time of year, and the !Kung may converge on the larger summer pans that still hold water. Food is abundant, with plenty of the summer berries and melons still available. The April mongongo nut harvest puts a major new food into the diet.

!Gum (winter)   The cool dry season extends from the end of May through August. It is heralded by a sharp drop in nightly temperatures, with the peak cold in late June. In 1968, Dobe experienced a month or more of freezing and near-freezing nights. The !Kung winter camps, usually around a permanent waterhole, are well stocked with firewood to burn through the cold nights. Fortunately, the days are crisp, clear, and warm. The diet is varied during the winter months. Mongongo fruit and nut, baobab, and many species of roots and bulbs provide the staples. The clear, pleasant days are ideal for walking; winter is a time for visiting relatives at distant camps. The good tracking conditions encourage more

hunting and the setting up of snarelines. As the season passes, plant foods become increasingly scare as foods are eaten up in wider and wider radii around the permanent waterholes.

!Gaa (spring dry season)   The final season of the !Kung year begins in late August with a rapid increase in daily temperatures and ends in October or early November with the onset of the first rains. This is the least attractive time of year. Although humidity remains low, the days are exceedingly hot, with highs from 33 to 43 degrees Centigrade (92 to 110 degrees Fahrenheit) in the shade. Work is difficult, and the better foods may be available only at distances from camp. It is in this season that the !Kung make use of the widest variety of plant foods. Fibrous roots, ignored at other times, may be dug and eaten without enthusiasm. Hunting, however, can be very good at this time of year due to the weakness of the animals. The !Kung eagerly await the onset of the next rainfall and the new season of plenty.

Rainfall is concentrated in the hot summer months (October to May), and from June to September the Dobe area is completely dry. The most striking fact, however, is the enormous yearly variation in amount and distribution of rainfall. Figure 3–2 shows the rainfall at Dobe for two rainy seasons and most of a third. Rainfall varied from 239 millimeters in the drought of 1963–1964 to 597 millimeters in the good year of 1967–1968, a swing of 250 percent (from 10 to 24 inches). Month-to-month and place-to-place variations further increase the uncertainty of precipitation.

Droughts are frequent. At Maun (the nearest weather station to Dobe with long-term records), drought occurs two years out of every five, and severe drought occurs about one year in four.[1] With a lower average rainfall, the situation at Dobe would be, if not worse, at least no better than the situation at Maun (Lee 1972b).

Too *much* rainfall can also present a problem. Superrecord rains fell in 1973–1974 (1184 millimeters or 47 inches at Maun) and seriously reduced the mongongo crop, although the crop recovered the following year.

The message of the foregoing discussion is clear. There is no such thing as a typical rainfall year for the !Kung. They must continuously adapt their subsistence strategy to high-rainfall years, to low-rainfall years, and to marked local variability. Theirs is long-term adaptation to the problem of living: the ethnographer sees only a small segment of the overall pattern in a given year of fieldwork. This theme will crop up again as we explore the !Kung way of life in more depth (for example, see Chapter 7 on *Hxaro* Exchange).

SETTLEMENT PATTERNS

The !Kung word for village or camp, *chu/o*, means literally "the face of the huts." The *chu/o* symbolizes for the !Kung the safety, comfort, and companionship

---

[1] Severe drought occurs when annual rainfall is less than 70 percent of average.

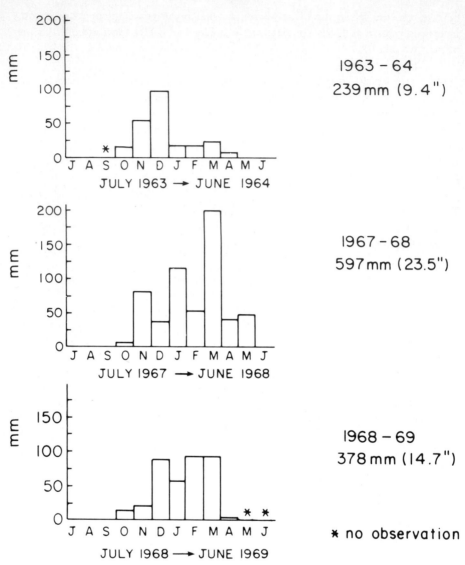

Figure 3–2. Rainfall at Dobe for three years.

of the group, and the term is contrasted in their thought with the term *t'si*, meaning "bush" or wilderness. *Chu/o* is tamed space, cultural space; *t'si* is untamed or natural space.[2]

A typical !Kung camp is a rough circle of grass huts some 10 to 30 meters (30

---

[2] Unlike the Mbuti pygmies, who revere the forest, the !Kung do not express reverence or even much affection for the semiarid savannah that surrounds them. They know it intimately, derive all their economic needs from it, and are comfortable traveling through it, but they do not deify it or attribute any supernatural powers to the land *per se* (see Chapter 8).

to 100 feet) in diameter, arranged around a central clearing. This section discusses the settlement patterns of the !Kung under the following headings:

1. Village Types
2. The Layout of the Camp
3. Hut and Shelter Construction
4. Ethnoarcheology

Village Types

Mobility is the essence of the !Kung adaptation. This factor strongly influences the settlement pattern. !Kung villages are easily established and moved frequently. Habitations are built in a few hours or a few days, and camp sites are rarely occupied for more than a few months before being abandoned. In all, five types of villages and camps can be usefully distinguished.

A. Dry season villages   These sites, occupied for 3 to 6 months from May or June to September or October, are fairly large, often containing 8 to 15 huts and 20 to 50 people. They are always located near permanent water sources and, because of their accessibility (to outsiders) and their long duration, are by far the most thoroughly studied of all the !Kung village types. Dry season huts tend to be well-constructed; the site is cleared with care, and large middens of garbage accumulate before the site is abandoned. As a result, the archeological visibility of the dry season camps is highest of all the settlement types.

B. Rainy season villages   These are located near major seasonal water and food sources. They are highly variable in size (from 3 to 20 huts) and are usually occupied for periods of three weeks to three months. The site is casually cleared,

A rainy season camp in the Mongongo groves.

and the huts are hastily constructed, though thickly thatched in order to provide shelter from the rains. When these are abandoned the saplings used in hut construction may be moved to the next locale. A group may occupy as many as six sites in the course of a single rainy season.

C. Spring and fall camps These are called camps rather than villages; because of the dry weather no huts are built, and they are rarely occupied for more than two or three weeks. Under certain circumstances similar short-term camps may also be established in summer when the group is moving from the foraging area to another, or in the winter when a group is taking advantage of a still-available seasonal water source.

D. Overnight stops These are what the name implies. Only a fire is built, and the site is abandoned the next morning. Overnight stops occur in all seasons.

E. Cattle post villages These new-style villages have became increasingly common since 1970. They involve solid, carefully constructed huts, usually built on sites close to an Herero or Tswana village. The size of these villages varies from one to twenty huts, but common to all is a crescent-shaped (not circular) layout around a central cattle kraal, with hut mouths facing the cattle compound rather than each other. This shift in layout sums up a key symbolic shift in social orientation. Whereas the older camps were circular so that the !Kung could look at each other, the cattle-post !Kung now look to the livestock for their survival. Another prominent feature of these villages is their long duration; some are still occupied 18 to 20 years after being built.

The Layout of the Camp

Choosing a site is not a great problem for the !Kung. They look for good shade trees in an area that has not been too recently occupied. They do not return again and again to the same spot, so there is not much opportunity for a great residue of artifacts to build up. They live lightly on the land.

The village site itself can be seen as consisting of five concentric circles, each with a different function (Fig. 3–3). In the center lies the village's public space, a cleared "plaza" from 5 to 25 meters (15 to 75 feet) in diameter where children play and people may gather, and where in the evening healing dances are held. Around the central area is the most important part of the village, the ring of huts —*chutsi-* —and hearths—*datsi-*. Each woman builds her hut with a space of 3 to 5 meters from those of her neighbors. Directly in front of the hut mouth is the family fire, at which all the food is cooked, where people socialize in the evening, and around which the family sleeps at night. The space immediately around the hut and fire is carefully cleared of all grass and shrubs so that people can move about easily day or night, without fear of poisonous snakes or scorpions.

Most villages exhibit a symbolic order, with the most senior household situated on the side of the village from which its ancestors were said to have come and with its married children's huts strung out to the right and left. Other senior households and in-law segments usually situate themselves opposite the most senior

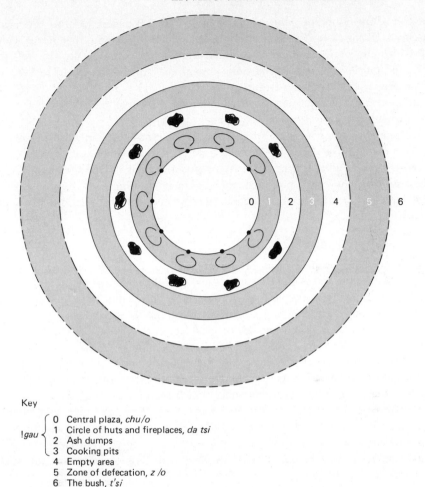

Key

!gau
{
0 Central plaza, *chu/o*
1 Circle of huts and fireplaces, *da tsi*
2 Ash dumps
3 Cooking pits
}
4 Empty area
5 Zone of defecation, *z /o*
6 The bush, *t'si*

Figure 3–3. Idealized plan of a !Kung village (chu/o).

couple, with their offspring strung out to their right and left, and thus a circle is constituted (see also Marshall 1960).

The next ring, about 5 meters deep immediately behind the huts, is the zone of ash heaps and garbage dumps. Every ten days or so !Kung women clean out their hearths and dump the ashes and nut-shells behind their huts. In a six-month camp, middens up to half a meter (20 inches) in height will accumulate and the fireplace in turn may be scooped out so that it gradually sinks a foot below grade.

The third ring, about 25 meters (80 feet) deep, is the zone where cooking pits are dug. Whenever a large animal is killed, the head is cooked separately by digging a 2-foot-deep pit, filling it with burning wood, placing the head on top of the fire, then adding more embers and wood, and covering it with sand. After two hours of cooking the meat is served. Butchery of large animals and emptying and cleaning of entrails is also carried out here.

The last ring in the cultural space is the area of defecation, *z/o*. Depending on the size of the camp, this zone can be from 100 to 300 meters (350 to 1000 feet) in depth. !Kung have no latrines or privies, and they distribute themselves widely when carrying out their toilet. The abundant Kalahari dung beetles that roll into balls and quickly carry away and bury human and animal feces help to keep the z/o relatively clean and odor-free.

Beyond this outer perimeter, paths radiate outward into the t'si itself, the wild lands of subsistence into which the foragers venture.

Despite the !Kung imagery of the t'si as wilderness, and in spite of the real dangers that lurk in t'si, it is extremely interesting and significant that the traditional !Kung did not attempt to fortify or stockade their village sites in any way.[3] They sleep in the open, protected only by their sleeping fires, which keep the carnivores at bay, and by their mutual trust of and peaceful relations with their human neighbors.

Hut and Shelter Construction

A !Kung rainy season hut can be constructed in a day. A dry season hut, to last for several months, takes three or four days to build. First, 10 to 12 saplings are cut, and each is dug in vertically in a circle with an opening for the mouth. The tops are tied together to form a dome, and the frame is strengthened horizontally with pliable branches. Then bundles of grass are cut and transported back to the site, where handfuls of thatch are carefully woven into the frame to form the walls. In the rainy season the top of the hut is heavily thatched to protect against the elements. In the dry season the dome of the hut is left open to catch the warming sun. People do not live in their huts, which are only 2 to 2.5 meters (6 to 8 feet) wide and less than 2 meters (6.5 feet) high. They use them as a place to store their belongings, as a windbreak and a place for an afternoon nap, and as a symbolic element to structure the living space. Since they are composed of organic materials, !Kung huts become quickly infested with bugs and are not particularly pleasant places to be in.

Three other kinds of structures are built in !Kung villages: tree storage areas, storage platforms, and meat-drying racks. For the first, a nest of branches and thatch is built at chest height in the crotch of a convenient tree. Men store their arrow poison out of reach of children, dried strips of biltong out of reach of dogs, and other valuables out of sight of the inquisitive eyes of neighbors.

The storage platform, built on four poles, serves the same function, with the additional advantage of casting a pool of shade for conversation. The drying rack is built if a large kill provides more meat than can be locally consumed.

In recent years the !Kung have been abandoning their beehive-shaped grass huts in favor of the more substantial Tswana-style house with a vertical pole and mud walls, a mud floor, and a separate thatched roof. These huts take weeks or months to build, and when one is completed its owner is not likely to want to leave it soon. Many of these new-style huts are occupied continuously for years and mark the dramatic transition to sedentary life.

---

[3] Only since the arrival of cattle have some villages put up a rough stockade to keep the animals from eating their thatching and other articles (see Chapter 9).

Ethnoarcheology

Until recently, !Kung life in the Dobe area constituted an endless cycle of seasonal movement, with each group building and abandoning three to six villages each year. These abandoned villages—//*gung*/*osi*—form an important part of the social landscape. Each permanent waterhole is surrounded by dozens of them, and most adults can point to the campsites of their childhood. With the passing of the generations, gradually the campsites fade from human memory, become buried in the sand, and are converted into archeological sites.

The fact that !Kung village sites of the 1960s strongly resemble the village sites of prehistoric foragers 100 to 500 or more years old offers us two kinds of important data. First, it shows us the continuity of the living cultures of the Dobe area with those of the past, and second, it offers us the chance to use the behaviors of the living as an aid to the interpretation of the past. The new science of *ethnoarcheology* does precisely this: the foraging behavior of living people is observed and then the material residues of that behavior are plotted. The residues produced by known behaviors are then compared with archeological residues for which the behaviors are not known.

Underlying ethnoarcheology is an assumption of uniformitarianism.[4] The same processes that produce the campsites of contemporary !Kung are postulated to have been instrumental in producing the campsites of prehistoric foragers. For example, if a group of 20 occupies a camp for 14 days and leaves a residue of 20 cubic meters of nutshells, and the same group's occupation of 28 days leaves 40 cubic meters, what length of stay would we expect to find for a residue of 60 cubic meters, of 10 cubic meters, and so on? This is one kind of question that ethnoarcheology seeks to answer.[5]

John Yellen, Alison Brooks, and others have been doing ethnoarcheology research on the !Kung for 15 years. Readers wishing to find out more about this approach are encouraged to consult their work (Yellen 1977; Brooks and Yellen 1979, 1981).

---

[4] A term coined by the great nineteenth-century geologist and friend of Darwin, Charles Lyell (1793–1867).

[5] If you answered 42 days and 7 days, you were correct. Of course the same volume of residue could be produced by a larger group staying for a shorter period; for example, a residue of 60 cubic meters could be produced by a group of 42 staying 20 days.

4 / Subsistence: foraging for a living

The morning after I arrived in Dobe and before I had even set up my camp, my new-found neighbors came to me with a proposition. N!eishi and his son ≠Toma approached me and said, "There is no food in our camp and we are hungry, would the bearded White man take us in his truck to get some food?"

"Isn't there any food around here?" I asked through the interpreter.

"There is some," the answer came back. "A few bitter roots and berries. But we want to show you a place where the food is good and there is plenty."

"But what kind of food?" I asked, reaching for my notebook.

"//gxa," ≠Toma said. "The Tswanas call it mongongo."

I had heard about mongongo, from reading the Marshall research (they called it *mangetti*, the Herero name for it), and the Dobe camp was littered with mounds of empty nutshells. I was keen to see what the trees looked like. A trip there would also put me on good terms with my neighbors.

"How far is it?" I asked, not wanting to get involved in a wild-goose chase.

"Oh, it's not far," N!eishi and ≠Toma assured me. "We'll be there in no time."

Just as the truck started, six women from Dobe camp rushed forward and asked if they could come too. They hopped onto the back, and as we set out they broke out in a song, a rousing chorus with a pleasant melody sung in complex rhythms. I later learned that this was the truck song (*dotsi*), sung whenever the !Kung got a lift on one. The joyous words to celebrate the luxury of high-speed transportation go something like this: "*do si bereka, moseliseliyana*" (while the truck does the work we sit around and get fat).

I also liked the lyric to another verse that went "Those who work for a living, that's their problem!" Despite the song, the travel was anything but high-speed, and our destination was anything but near. We ground along for hours in four-wheel drive at a walking pace where no truck had ever been before, swerving to avoid antbear holes and circumventing fallen trees.

At several points along the way I spotted trees that looked familiar.

"Isn't that a mongongo tree?" I asked. "And what are those little nuts lying on the ground?"

"Yes, that's mongongo, all right," ≠Toma replied, "but those groves are almost finished. Keep going."

It was noon before ≠Toma signaled that we had reached our destination. It was worth waiting for. We stood on the top of the dune in the middle of a large grove

34

of mongongo trees that stretched east and west to the horizon. The fallen nuts densely covered the ground. This was a fresh grove, unpicked this season. I reckoned we were about ten miles north of Dobe.

Without ceremony, the women fanned out and started to pick. Grabbing my camera, stopwatch, and notebook, I hastened to follow them. They bent from the waist with a smooth and effortless motion and picked 5 or 6 nuts each time and popped them in their *karosses*, one-piece garments-*cum*-carrying-bags. Every ten minutes or so, each would return to the truck to spill out her load on the spot she had picked out. The individual piles began to accumulate rapidly. The men were collecting too, using smaller bags than those of the women. I sampled how rapidly the women were able to pick. They were gathering at the rate of 40 to 60 nuts per minute, or 2000 to 3000 nuts per hour. By two o'clock everyone was finished; they dumped their final few onto the piles, which looked enormous to me. The women took off their *karosses* and laid them flat. After piling all their nuts into the middle of the *karosses*, they made manageable bundles of them by bringing the four corners together and sewing the edges together with bark stripped from a nearby tree. Some women used pieces of storebought cloth to make their bundles. Some stopped to crack a few nuts with stones they found nearby and eat them as they waited for the others to finish.

The bundles were loaded on the truck, which, with the eight people, was riding dangerously low. We set off on our return journey, arriving home before nightfall.

I was curious to see just how much food had been gathered in the short time

Tin!kay packing mongongo nuts at !Gausha.

we had been in the groves. A simple fisherman's scale gave a rough-and-ready answer. The women's loads weighed 30 to 50 pounds each, and the men's 15 to 25 pounds each. That worked out to about 23,000 calories of food for each woman collector, and 12,000 for each man. Each woman had gathered enough to feed a person for 10 days and each man enough for 5 days. Not at all a bad haul for 2 hours' work!

My first full day of fieldwork had already taught me to question one popular view of hunter-gatherer subsistence: that life among these people was precarious, a constant struggle for existence. My later studies were to show that the !Kung in fact enjoyed a rather good diet and that they didn't have to work very hard to get it. As we will see, even without the aid of an anthropologist's truck the !Kung had to work only 20 hours a week in subsistence. But what about the fact that N!eishi had come to me that morning saying that they were hungry and that there was no food nearby? Strictly speaking, N!eishi spoke the truth. October is one of the harder months of the year, at the end of the dry season, and the more desirable foods had been eaten out close to Dobe. What N!eishi did not say was that a little farther away food *was* available, and, if not plentiful, there was enough to see them through until the rains came. When N!eishi came to me with his propo-

The mongongo.

sition, he was making an intelligent use of his resources, social and otherwise. Why hike in the hot sun for a small meal, when the bearded White man might take you in his truck for ten large ones?

The security of the !Kung life is attributable mainly to the fact that vegetable food and not meat forms the mainstay of their diet. Plant foods are abundant, locally available, and predictable; game animals, in contrast, are scarce and unpredictable. In addition to the mongongo nut, the !Kung have an astonishing inventory of over 100 edible plants: 14 fruits and nuts, 15 berries, 18 species of edible gum, 41 edible roots and bulbs, and 17 leafy greens, beans, melons, and other foods: 105 species in all. The abundance and variety of plant foods makes it possible for the !Kung to feed themselves by an average of about 20 hours of subsistence work per adult per week, a far lower figure than the 40-hour work week we have come to accept in the industrialized countries. In this chapter we explore how this "affluent" way of life is achieved by the !Kung in their harsh, semiarid desert environment.

GATHERING AND CARRYING

The tools and techniques of gathering are relatively simple. The knowledge of plant identification, growth, ripeness, and location, however, is extremely complex, and the !Kung women are highly skilled at distinguishing useful from nonuseful or dangerous plants and at finding and bringing home sufficient quantities of the best food species available.

Only a single tool, the digging stick, is used in gathering. Carrying, on the other hand, involves the use of several ingenious multipurpose containers and an elaborate body of knowledge.

The versatile digging stick is used to dig out roots and bulbs; it is also used in hunting to dig burrowing mammals, in water-getting to dig out water-bearing roots, and as a carrying device to transport large roots impaled on it or suspended from it with twine. For the remaining nonroot 75 percent of the vegetable diet—fruits, nuts, gums, melons, and leafy greens—no special gathering tools are used.

Carrying Devices
The kaross Foremost among the carrying devices is the woman's kaross (*chi !kan*), a formidable one-piece combination garment-*cum*-carrying device that also does service as a sleeping blanket (Figure 4–1). The men manufacture these for the women from the hides of the female kudu, gemsbok, wildebeest, or eland. This suede garment is worn draped over the wearer's back. Tied at the waist with a leather thong, the lower half of the kaross conceals the wearer's backside, and the upper half forms a pouch for carrying vegetables, water containers, firewood, and babies. With a center of gravity close to the body, the kaross is ideal for carrying heavy loads. In !Kung thought, the kaross is so characteristic of women and their work that the knot (*!kebi*) that ties the kaross at a woman's waist is also an affectionate colloquial term for "women" (*!kebisi*).

Leather bags A variety of sturdy leather bags are made from the skins of the steenbok and duiker. Both men and women wear small "handbags" over the

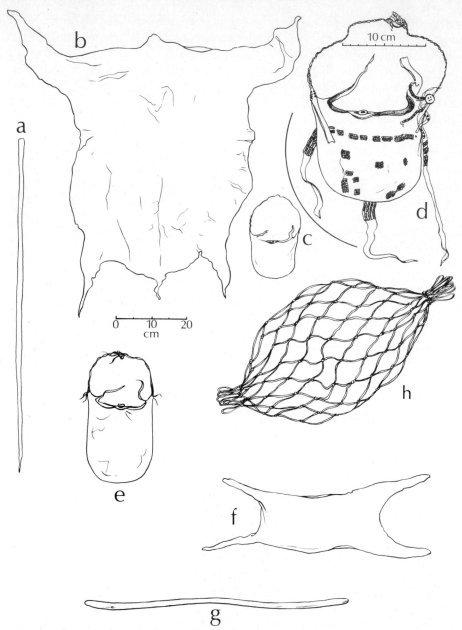

Figure 4–1. Gathering and carrying equipment: (a) digging stick; (b) kaross;
(c) small bag; (d) small bag (detailed); (e) man's bag; (f) baby carrier;
(g) carrying yoke; (h) man's net.

shoulder and under the armpit for keeping handy tobacco, fire-making kits, sewing
materials, and other items. The women's bags are brightly decorated with beadwork.
For carrying foodstuffs and larger items, large bags called / *tausi* are used, ranging
up to the size of a grocery shopping bag.

Women carrying loads in their karosses.

Baby sling For carrying a young infant, a mother employs a special leather baby carrier, tied around her waist and over her shoulders, that fits inside the kaross on her hip and allows the baby access to the breast (Figure 4–1). This special baby carrier is lined with soft grasses and other absorbent materials and is frequently cleaned and aired. When an older, toilet-trained child is carried, he or she sits directly in the main pouch of the kaross or is carried on the shoulder by a woman or man.

Carrying net Men make an ingeniously intricate knotted net, called /wisi, for use as a carrying device (Figure 4–1). This wide-meshed net, 100 centimeters (3 feet) long and 40 centimeters (16 inches) across, can be lined with long grass and used to carry quantities of such small items as nuts and berries.

Carrying yoke The carrying yoke (!garo) is easily made from a rough wooden branch. Full bags, nets, bundles of meat, and haunches of freshly killed game are slung from either end, and the load is shouldered by a man for the long trips between camps.

Because the essence of the !Kung adaptation is mobility, and because their daily diet consists mostly of hundreds of small nuts, berries, and roots, San life would not be possible without means of carrying quantities of these small foods back to the camp or home base. !Kung carrying technology is well developed and well designed. A similar degree of development is reflected in their vocabulary, which has a multitude of terms for different ways of carrying. A partial list is shown in Table 4.1 and illustrated in Figure 4–2. One cannot overstate the im-

TABLE 4–1   CARRYING VOCABULARY (SEE FIGURE 4–2 FOR ILLUSTRATIONS).

To Carry on the Back		To Carry Otherwise	
1. A child	*maa*	11. On the head	*ku≠tem*
2. A load (males)	*//xam*	12. On the belt	*!uu*
3. A load (females)	*//kei*	13. To drag (not shown)	*!gwe*
4. A *kaross* package	*!guu*	14. To carry firewood in a *kaross*	*!gaba*
To Carry on the Shoulders		**To Carry with a Carrying Yoke**	
5. A child	*chi*	15. To stick a load through (not shown)	*/di*
6. An object	*!kai*	16. to hang a load from	*//gau*
7. A bag or quiver	*!wana*	17. To impale a root and carry	*n!n//xam*
8. A carrying yoke	*//wana*		*du tsiu*
9. A *kaross*	*//gama*	18. To carry with two carrying yokes	*!garo*
10. A spear	*!kei//kun*		

portance of carrying and carrying devices for San life and for the life of hunting and gathering peoples in general. The universality of the carrying device and its functional importance among all recent hunter-gatherers has implications for the evolution of human subsistence during the Pleistocene, because a device for carrying vegetable foods would seem to be a prerequisite for human economic and social life (see Lee 1979:489–494).

Major and Minor Foods[1]

Over 100 species of wild plants are classified by the !Kung as edible. However, not all plant foods are valued equally. Some are prized and eaten daily; others are despised and rarely eaten. Complex criteria are applied by the !Kung to arrange their plant foods into a hierarchy of classes of desirability. Abundance, duration of eating season, ease of collecting, tastiness, absence of side effects, and nutritional value are six of the criteria !Kung use to classify their food as */gau* (strong) or */ta/tana* (weak) foods. To their own judgments I have added my observations on frequency of eating and quantities eaten and have drawn up a six-class hierarchy of foods:

Food Classes:		Criteria:
1. Primary	1 species	widely abundant year-round
2. Major	13 species	widely abundant
3. Minor	19 species	locally seasonally abundant
4. Supplementary	30 species	locally seasonally available
5. Rare	19 species	rarely observed to be eaten
6. Problematic	23 species	!Kung classify as edible; not observed to be eaten

[1] The research on which this discussion is based was carried out in 1963–1969. In the 1970s, models of optimal foraging strategy began to be widely applied to gathering and hunting humans (e.g., Winterhalder and Smith 1981). The discussion presented here closely anticipates the spirit and underlying assumptions of optimal foraging theory, although I have several points of disagreement with optimal foraging as currently applied to humans.

Cooking the fruit of the mongongo.

The mongongo (fruit and nut) is in a class by itself. All the Dobe !Kung agree that it is their most important vegetable food. It is superabundant, found near all waterholes, and available in all months of the year; it is easy to collect, tasty, and highly nutritious. Only meat rivals the mongongo as the most desirable food of the

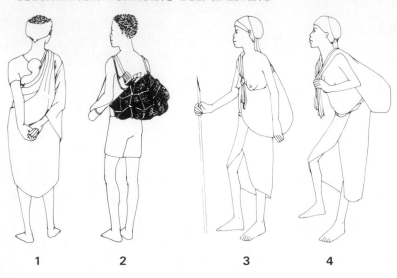

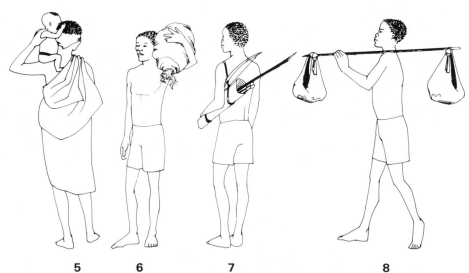

Figure 4–2. !Kung carrying positions (for explanation, see Table 4–1).

!Kung. I asked one informant to tell me what his idea of an ideal diet would consist of. Without hesitation, he listed four items: meat and mongongo for strength, honey for sweetness, and wild orange fruits for refreshment.

Thirteen additional species are considered major foods. These are rated high on most, but not all, the criteria of desirability. Most are seasonal and therefore

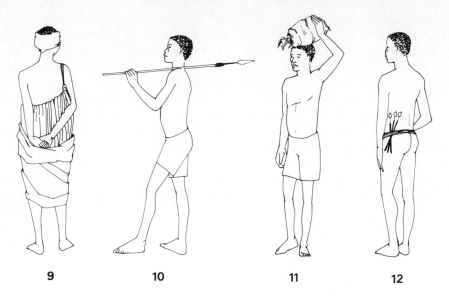

9   10   11   12

14   17   18   16

not available year-round, and most are not universally distributed at all the waterholes. All are abundant, and each may exceed the mongongo in importance at certain waterholes at certain times of the year. Baobab, for example, is tasty and abundant but is mainly concentrated in a few waterholes such as !Kubi and is rare or absent at others. Marula is found at most of the waterholes, but its nut-meat is smaller than that of mongongo, and its shell is harder to crack.

Nineteen of the species are listed as minor foods; these rate high on one or two criteria of desirability. Included are seven species of roots and bulbs that, taken individually, are not important, but that as a group become a major item of the diet during the winter dry season, when the major summer foods are not available. All the species of class III are seasonally limited.

The largest class is supplementary foods, with 30 species. As the name implies, these foods supplement the foods in classes I, II, and III or are eaten when the more desirable foods become locally exhausted. The list includes 6 species of fruits and berries, 10 of edible gum, 12 roots and bulbs, a bean, and a leafy green. In general, the foods of class IV are both less abundant and less tasty than the corresponding foods of class III.

The rare foods (19 species) were observed to be eaten on only a few occasions each year. Many were quite scarce; others were plentiful but were downgraded because of poor taste or undesirable side effects.

Finally, there are the 23 species listed as problematic foods. The !Kung said that these were edible, but I did not observe them to be eaten during the study period.

Food Classes and Subsistence Strategy

The way the !Kung hierarchically evaluate their plant inventory in order of importance as food suggests a productive analogy to the way they utilize space in the short run in subsistence activities. The !Kung typically occupy a campsite for a period of weeks and eat their way out of it. For instance, at a camp in the mongongo forest the members exhaust the nuts within a 1.5-kilometer (1-mile) radius the first week of occupation, within a 3-kilometer (2-mile) radius the second week, and within a 5-kilometer (3-mile) radius the third week. The longer a group lives at a camp, the farther it must travel each day to get food. This feature of daily subsistence characterizes both summer and winter camps. For example, at the Dobe winter camp in June 1964 the gatherers were making daily round trips of 9 to 14 kilometers to reach the mongongo groves. By August the daily round trips had increased to 19 kilometers.

This progressive increase in walking distance occurs because the !Kung are highly selective in their food habits. They do not eat *all* the food in a given area. They start by eating out the most desirable species, and when these are exhausted or depleted they turn to the less desirable species. Because plant food resources are both varied and abundant, in any situation where the desirable foods are scarce, the !Kung have two alternatives in food strategy: (1) they may walk farther in order to obtain the more desirable species, or (2) they may remain closer to camp and exploit the less desirable species. In fact, both alternatives are practiced simultaneously: the younger, more active camp members go farther afield to bring back foods of classes I and II, and the older, more sedentary camp members collect class III and IV foods closer to home. Because the day's foods are pooled within families and shared out to other families at adjacent fires, the net effect is that every camp member has a variety of food available at the end of the day— and no one goes hungry.

HUNTING

Though vegetable foods provide the bulk of the diet, we should not underestimate the returns from hunting. Meat contributes about 30 percent of the calories to the diet and hunting was the major occupation of the men, up to about 1970. All !Kung, men and women alike, rate meat among their most valued foods. Part of its value comes from its scarcity. Steak is always better than potatoes. But its social value is, I think, paramount. Whenever a large animal is killed it is the occasion for feasting. Great cauldrons of meat are cooked round-the-clock, and people gather from far and wide to eat. Distribution is done with great care, according to a set of rules, arranging and rearranging the pieces for up to an hour so that each recipient will get the right proportion. Successful distributions are remembered with pleasure for weeks afterwards, while improper meat distributions can be the cause of bitter wrangling among close relatives.

Tools and Techniques

The hunting weaponry consists of major tools and minor ones. The major ones are the bow and arrow, spear, knife, springhare hook, and rope snares (see Figure 4–3). The minor tools include digging stick and fire-making equipment. In addi-

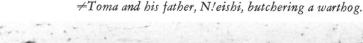

≠Toma and his father, N!eishi, butchering a warthog.

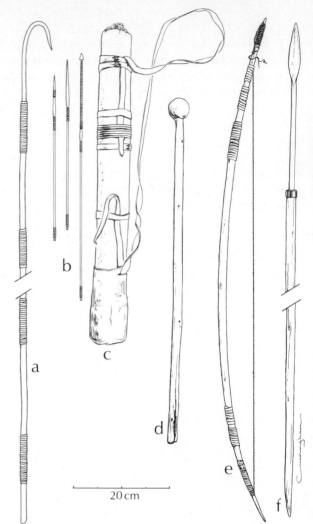

Figure 4–3. !Kung hunting weapons: (a) springhare probe; (b) arrows; (c) quiver; (d) club; (e) bow; (f) spear.

20 cm

tion, knife, ropes, and carrying yoke are used in butchery and in carrying the meat back to camp. Guns are almost entirely absent in Dobe !Kung hunting. Though some men had hunted with guns borrowed from the Herero, only one man out of 151 !Kung owned a gun and used it for hunting while I was there.

The !Kung have four types of hunting techniques. First is the mobile hunt, with bow and poisoned arrows, for plains game such as kudu and gemsbok and wildebeeste. This is the kind of hunting most outsiders associate with the !Kung and other hunting peoples (see John Marshall's film "The Hunters"). It may surprise some that the other hunting techniques produce many more kills than the classic bow-and-arrow hunt.

Hunting with dogs is the second kind of hunt. Warthog, steenbok, duiker, and hares are taken this way. Well-trained hunting dogs bring small game to bay, and the hunter finishes it off with a spear. N!eishi's son ≠Toma had a famous pair of dogs named Swoiya and Foiya, with which he killed warthog at the rate of three per month.

I was surprised to find that the !Kung do much of their hunting *underground*, pursuing burrowing animals into their lairs. Antbear, warthog, and porcupine are taken this way. The latter two are hunted above ground as well. The nocturnal springhare sleeps in narrow burrows during the day. !Kung hunters have developed a special tool, a thirteen-foot-long pole with an iron hook at the end, for probing springhare burrows and impaling the animals underground. The burrow is then excavated with a digging stick to retrieve the kill. This is hot, dusty work, which the !Kung were only too glad to turn over to the visiting anthropologist.

The fourth technique is snaring, employed particularly by older hunters whose mobility is limited. A man surveys an area of bush for fresh tracks, then he lays down an unobstrusive line of brush to accustom the animals to cross at certain gaps. The snares are made of rope from local fiber plants with a delicate wooden trigger attached to a bent-over sapling. When the hare, guinea fowl, or small antelope steps in the snare, the noose tightens and the sapling springs up, leaving the quarry dangling. Snaring does not produce a large quantity of meat. In July 1964 at Dobe, 18 animals were killed, 11 of them by snares. These 11, however, provided only 20 percent of the meat of the camp.

The Joys of Tracking

The !Kung are such superb trackers and make such accurate deductions from the faintest marks in the sand that at first their skill seems uncanny. For example, both men and women are able to identify an individual person merely by the sight of his or her footprint in the sand. There is nothing mysterious about this. Their tracking is a skill, cultivated over a lifetime, that builds on literally tens of thousands of observations. The !Kung hunter can deduce many kinds of information about the animal he is tracking: its species and sex, its age, how fast it is traveling, whether it is alone or with other animals, its physical condition (healthy or ill), whether and on what it is feeding, and the time of the day the animal passed this way.

The species, of course, is identified by the shape of the hoofprint and by the dung or scat; this is the simplest information to be deduced, and any 12-year-old boy can accurately reproduce in the sand the prints of a dozen species. The size or age of an animal correlates directly with the size of its print. The depth of the print indicates the weight of the animal. An old or infirm animal may be distinguished by a halting gait or uneven stride length. Evidence of crippling is eagerly sought and is discerned when one hoofprint is deeper than the others.

Knowledge of the animal's habits aids in determining the time of day it passed by. Some of the signs are surprisingly simple. If the tracks zigzag from shade tree to tree, the animal went through the heat of the day. If the tracks go under the west side of the trees, the animal was catching the morning shade; if under the east side, the afternoon shade; and if under either side, the animal passed at midday. Milling tracks within a small radius out in the open suggest that the animal was there at night and was sleeping. Tracks leading into a dense thicket indicate the animal rested up during midday.

Perhaps the most amazing skill is in the hunter's ability to figure out the number of minutes or hours elapsed since the animal went through. This is crucial information; to obtain it, the !Kung have developed their discriminating powers to the highest degree. After a print has been made, it provides a miniature physiographic feature that is acted upon by natural processes. Consider a simple example. When fresh, the print is clean-cut, but after an hour (or less, if the day is windy) a fine covering of windblown sand collects in the depression. Later, twigs and grass fall in, and then insect and other animal tracks are superimposed. The moisture content of the soil 1, 2, 3, or 4 centimeters below the surface and the rate at which soil dries out after being exposed by a footfall are two variables that are exceedingly well studied by the !Kung. When an animal is being closely followed, the present position of the shade in relation to the animal's footprint plus these other signs can indicate to within 15 minutes the time the animal passed by.

All these kinds of information and more are interpreted by the hunter in order to decide whether a trail is worth pursuing or not. Ideally, a hunter looks for an older or infirm animal moving slowly in thick brush. The hunter then can creep up to get within firing range while the quarry is unaware. A final stalk may take up to 40 minutes, with the hunter creeping on his elbows and knees. To have a reasonable chance of placing an arrow, the hunter should be within 100 feet.

Once the animal is hit, the poison must do its work. Well placed, a poisoned arrow can kill a large antelope within 6 to 24 hours. After the hunter examines the tracks for signs of blood, he does a surprising thing: he goes home. There is no point chasing an animal to its death place, which could be miles away. Instead, the hunter heads back to camp for the night. In the morning the hunter, accompained by a party of carriers, goes out to pick up the wounded animal's trail. They follow the prey to its place of dying, butcher the carcass, and bring it home.

Not all hunts are successful. In fact, on most days of hunting a man will come back empty-handed. And even if an animal is wounded, there is no guarantee that the meat will ever reach camp. As many as half the animals shot by the !Kung either recover from their wounds or run so far that they die out of range of the carrying party. An individual hunter is deemed fortunate if he kills as many as two large antelopes per year. Most of the meat consumed by the !Kung comes from hundreds of kills of smaller animals.

INSULTING THE MEAT

When a hunter returns from a successful hunt, or when meat is brought into a camp, one would think that this would be met with open glee and the hunter praised for his skill. Quite the contrary: the people often display indifference or negativity at the news of a successful kill, and I was surprised to see the low-key way in which the hunters would break the news of their success. /Xashe, an excellent hunter from /Xai/xai, put it this way:

When you come home empty-handed, you sleep and you say to yourself, "Oh, what have I done? What's the matter that I haven't killed?" Then the next morning you get up and without a word you go out and hunt again. This time you *do* kill something, and you come home. My *tsu* ("older kinsman") sees me and asks: "Well what did you see today?" "Tsutsu," I reply, "I didn't see anything."

I am sitting there with my head in my hands but my *tsu* comes back to me because he is a *zhu/twa*. "What do you mean you haven't killed anything? Can't you see that I'm dying of hunger?"

"Well, there might be something out there. I just might have scratched its elbow."

Then you say, as he smiles, "Why don't we go out in the morning and have a look." And so we two and others will bring home the meat together the next day.

Men are encouraged to hunt as well as they can, and the people are happy when meat is brought in, but the correct demeanor for the successful hunter is modesty and understatement. A /Xai/xai man named /Gaugo said:

Say that a man has been hunting. He must not come home and announce like a braggart, "I have killed a big one in the bush!" He must first sit down in silence until I or someone else comes up to his fire and asks, "What did you see today?" He replies quietly, "Ah, I'm no good for hunting. I saw nothing at all . . . maybe just a tiny one." Then I smile to myself because I know he has killed something big.

The theme of modesty is continued when the butchering and carrying party goes to fetch the kill the following day. Arriving at the site, the members of the carrying party loudly express their disappointment to the hunter:

You mean you have dragged us all the way out here to make us cart home your pile of bones? Oh, if I had known it was this thin I wouldn't have come.

People, to think I gave up a nice day in the shade for this. At home we may be hungry, but at least we have nice cool water to drink.

To these insults the hunter must not act offended; he should respond with self-demeaning words:

You're right, this one is not worth the effort; let's just cook the liver for strength and leave the rest for the hyenas. It's not too late to hunt today, and even a duiker or a steenbok would be better than this mess.

The party, of course, has no intentions of abandoning the kill. The heavy joking and derision are directed toward one goal: the leveling of potentially arrogant behavior in a successful hunter. The !Kung recognize the tendency toward arrogance (≠*twi*) in young men and take definite steps to combat it. As ≠Tomazho, the famous healer from /Xai/xai, put it:

When a young man kills much meat, he comes to think of himself as a chief or a big man, and he thinks of the rest of us as his servants or inferiors. We can't accept this. We refuse one who boasts, for someday his pride will make him kill somebody. So we always speak of his meat as worthless. In this way we cool his heart and make him gentle.

Insulting the meat is one of the central practices of the !Kung that serve to maintain egalitarianism. Even though some men are much better hunters than others, their behavior is molded by the group to minimize the tendency toward self-praise and to channel their energies into socially beneficial activities. As a result, the existence of differences in hunting prowess does not lead to a system of Big Men in which a few talented individuals tower over the others in terms of prestige.

I didn't really understand the importance of meat insulting until the !Kung tried it on me. Visiting anthropologists, I found, are not immune to the faults of arrogance and self-praise. One Christmas I planned to slaughter an ox as a way of saying thank you to the !Kung for their cooperation over the past year. The !Kung didn't see it that way and harassed me mercilessly in a way that was both hilarious and painful. The tale is told in a story called "Eating Christmas in the Kalahari," which is reproduced in the Appendix (pp. 151–156).

Though painful, the experience gave me a deeper insight into their core system of meaning. Insulting the meat is just one of a whole set of rough practices that allow the !Kung to sustain a sharing way of life (see also Chapter 7).

The theme of egalitarianism is also seen in several other hunting practices. Hunting magic and divination are frequently used to help a hunter who is down on his luck. And the widespread sharing of arrows also helps to reduce the considerable individual differences that exist in hunting ability.

The !Kung rule for allocating ownership of meat from a kill is "the owner of the arrow is the owner of the meat." Ownership here means primarily the right to distribute the meat. Men circulate arrows widely in the *hxaro* trade network. A man will say to another, "Give me an arrow, and if I kill something with it I will give the meat to you." Weeks or months later, when he kills an antelope, he shares the carcass with his trading partner if the latter happens to be in his camp. If the arrow-giver is elsewhere, the hunter saves a portion of the dried meat for him. This trading of arrows strengthens the bonds between men and is especially used between such kin categories as brothers-in-law. Women may own arrows too, trade them with men, and become owners of meat.

The reason for this high incidence of arrow sharing is not hard to find. A meat distribution brings prestige to the hunter, but it also can be a heavy burden, bringing with it the risk of accusations of stinginess or improper behavior if the distribution is not to everybody's liking. A practice that tends to diffuse the responsibility for meat distribution and spread the glory (and the hostility) around is therefore a blessing in such tense situations. Lorna Marshall makes this apt comment on the practice: "There is much giving and lending of arrows. The society seems to want to extinguish in every way possible the concept of the meat belonging to the hunter" (1976:297).

WORK EFFORT AND CALORIC RETURNS

As my research on the !Kung proceeded I was struck by the apparent lack of effort that went into the food quest. In the bush camps half or more of the adults seemed to be resting or sleeping in the camp on any given day. I had seen the abundance of mongongo nuts that the Dobe group had gathered the day after my arrival (see pp. 35–36), but didn't know whether this was a fluke made possible by the presence of my truck. I had learned to mistrust first impressions, and so I decided the only way to settle the issue was to make some systematic observations. How hard or easy was it to make a living? How many hours a day or days per week did the !Kung have to devote to subsistence activities? How adequate was their diet in meeting their nutritional needs? In July 1964 I started a daily work diary of the Dobe camp's activities. The whole camp was checked at sunrise and sunset to determine what each person was doing that day. The comings and goings of !Kung visitors were also recorded in order to establish a count of the number of mouths being fed each day. And the hunters were checked as they came home each day with or without meat. Women were monitored to see what species of plant foods they had gathered, and samples of their backloads were weighed on a simple scale.

July was neither the best nor the worst time of year for subsistence. The days were sunny and warm; the nights went down to freezing. Mongongo nuts were the major food, with smaller quantities of roots and bulbs. Berries, leafy greens, and other rainy-season foods were scarce or absent.

During the work study the population of the Dobe camp ranged from 23 to 40. On an average night there were 31 mouths to feed in the camp. I calculated work effort in terms of workweek, not because the !Kung think that way (they don't), but because it is a form that is easily understandable to us and makes possible comparison with other societies.[2]

At the end of four weeks I plotted out the figures (see Table 4–2). When the actual number of days of work was plotted, it turned out to be surprisingly low. From week to week the !Kung spent from 1.9 to 3.2 days in finding food. The overall average was 2.4 days of food-getting per person per week. Translated into hours, this worked out to about 20 hours of work per week, about half of the 40-hour-workweek that is standard in industrial societies.

Breaking down the figures by age and sex, I found that men worked more days per week than women, about 2.7 days for men compared to 2.1 days for women. Another interesting point was that though women did not hunt, men did gather: about one-fifth of all men's working days were spent in gathering and men's gathering accounted for about 22 percent of all the gathered foods. When I looked at the total contribution of all forms of activity to the diet, I saw that men provided about 45 percent of the food, and women 55 percent, even though men worked harder than women. Overall, vegetable foods provided 70 percent of the diet, and meat the other 30 percent.

How general was the low level of work seen at Dobe in July 1964? In 1969, Pat Draper studied work effort at seven foraging camps in the /Du/da area, 70 miles south of Dobe. She found that the workweek varied from 1.2 to 3.5 days, with an average of 2.3 days of work per week, very close to the Dobe average of 2.4 days (Draper, personal communication). Thus later studies at other water-holes showed that this leisurely pace of life was not unique to Dobe.

It would be misleading to leave the discussion of work effort here, since subsistence work is not the only kind of work the !Kung have to do. In addition,

[2] For a detailed discussion of methods and results, see Lee 1979:249–280.

TABLE 4–2   RESULTS OF THE DOBE WORK DIARY

| Week | Group Size | | Adult-Days | Child-Days | Total Person-Days of | | Work-Week | Meat Consumption | |
	Mean	Range			Consumption	Work		Kg.	lbs.
I (July 6–12)	25.6	23–29	114	65	179	37	2.3	42	92
II (July 13–19)	28.3	23–37	125	73	198	43	2.4	36	79
III (July 20–26)	34.3	29–40	156	84	240	42	1.9	80	176
IV (July 27–Aug. 2)	35.6	32–40	167	82	249	77	3.2	57.5	127
Total	30.9		562	304	866	199	2.4	215.5	474

TABLE 4–3   ESTIMATE OF OVERALL WORK EFFORT IN HOURS PER WEEK
FOR MEN AND WOMEN

	Subsistence Work	Tool Making and Fixing	Housework	Total Workweek (hours)
Men	21.6	7.5	15.4	44.5
Women	12.6	5.1	22.4	40.1
Average both sexes	17.1	6.3	18.9	42.3

there are the important tasks of manufacturing and maintaining their tool kit and, of course, housework—for the !Kung this involves food preparation, butchery, drawing water and gathering firewood, washing utensils, and cleaning the living space. These tasks take many hours a week. (But we should also remember that when Western economists calculate on-the-job work time, they do not include this type of work in their figures.)

The traditional !Kung make use of some 28 different tools and devices for gathering, hunting, cooking, and fetching water. In addition, their wardrobe consists of leather garments that have to be manufactured from the hides of game animals. They have to construct their houses, and their living and sleeping sites have to be cleared and maintained. These kinds of tasks add about an hour's work per day for men, and 45 minutes for women.[3] Finally, the tasks of housework, including an hour of nut-cracking per person per day, plus all the other tasks, add another 2 to 3 hours per day to the total work effort.

The overall estimate of hours per week shown in Table 4–3 is about 44.5 hours for men and 40.1 hours for women, with an overall average of 42.3 hours of work per person. This figure is still far below that level of work expected of people in our society. Studies have shown that North American wage-earners, those with many children especially, will spend up to 40 hours per week *over and above their wage-paid* job doing housework, shopping, washing, etc. This amount of work is not necessarily decreased by "labor-saving" washing machines and other appliances (Meissner *et al.* 1975:424–439).

The Quality and Quantity of the Diet

During the 28 days of the study the hunters brought in 18 animals yielding 454 pounds of meat, and gifts of meat from outside made up another 36 pounds of meat, for a total of 490 pounds. This works out to a daily consumption of 9.1 ounces of meat for every man, woman, and child. None of the kills were made with bow and poisoned arrows. ≠Toma, with his excellent hunting dogs, killed four warthogs, and these alone provided two-thirds of all the meat. Snaring and clubbing provided the remaining third of the meat.

Hunting success rates were not high. In all, seven men spent 78 man-days hunting. Since only 18 kills were made, it works out to only about 1 kill for every 4 man-days of hunting. Nevertheless, over a whole year, the average !Kung will

[3] The calculation of these figures is discussed in detail in Lee 1979:272–280.

TABLE 4–4   CALORIES AND PROTEINS IN THE !KUNG DIET.

Class of Food	Percent contribution to Diet by Weight	Per Capita Consumption		Calories/ Person/ Day
		Weight (g)	Protein (g)	
Meat	31	230	34.5	690
Mongongo nuts	28	210	58.8	1365
Other vegetables	41	300	3.0	300
Total	100	740	96.3	2355

consume between 175 and 200 pounds of meat, a very good level of nutrition by world standards, comparable to the level of meat consumption in the developed countries.

Although meat consumption was high, how adequately did the !Kung level of work effort meet their *overall* caloric needs? And did their diet provide them with the range of nutrients and minerals needed to maintain a healthy population? By weighing the food and calculating the nutrient composition I was able to come up with a rough estimate of the calories and proteins available in the daily diet. The figures are shown in Table 4–4.

Meat and mongongo nuts comprised the major part of the diet, contributing 31 and 28 percent of the weight respectively. About 20 species of roots, melons, gums, bulbs, and dried fruits, including some mongongo fruit, made up the remaining 41 percent of the diet. In all, the work of the !Kung made available a daily ration of 2355 calories of food energy and 96.3 grams of protein to each person. The diet was well-balanced in terms of vitamins and minerals, and if it was lacking anything it was an abundance of refined carbohydrates: there was no equivalent in the !Kung diet of the white bread, rice, pasta, and sugar-rich food that form so large a portion of our Western diet (and which may be responsible for our rapid growth rates). The caloric levels were more than adequate to support the Dobe population and to allow the people to live vigorous, active lives without losing weight.

The July work diary showed a good level of nutrition at one time of the year, a time of relative plenty. It was important to know how well people did at times of the year when food was scarcer. I did not collect work diary information at other times of year, but in a subsequent study Nancy Howell and I weighed people at various times of the year (Lee 1979:281–308). We reasoned as follows: though individual weights might vary, if overall weights remained fairly stable, that was a clear sign that nutrition was adequate. Conversely, if overall weights dipped sharply at one time of year, it would indicate a hungry season when the !Kung adaptation was put to the test.

In July 1968, Howell and I toured the Dobe area, stopping at all waterholes to weigh as many people as we could find. We repeated this weighing in October and again in January of 1969. In all, we were able to weigh 201 people in all three weight campaigns. The results showed that adult weights remained essentially stable from July to October, but dipped slightly from October to January, with a weight loss of 0.7 percent at Dobe and Mahopa and of 2.3 percent at /Xai/xai (Lee 1979:303). This loss of weight was statistically significant (it was not due to chance) but it was very small by the standards of other African societies, where seasonal weight losses of 6 or more percent were not uncommon.[4]

!KUNG SUBSISTENCE: AFFLUENCE OR ANXIETY?

The evidence from the study of seasonal weights therefore supported the evidence from the work and caloric studies. !Kung appeared to have the happy combination of an adequate diet and a short workweek. Over the course of a year, the picture of steady work, steady leisure, and adequate diet was maintained.

In summary, we have learned from the study of !Kung subsistence that despite the popular stereotypes, the !Kung do not have to work very hard to make a living. In assuming that their life must be a constant struggle for existence, we succumb to the ethnocentric notions that place our own Western adaptation at the pinnacle of success and make all others second or third best. Judged by these standards, the !Kung are bound to fail. But judged on their own terms, they do pretty well for themselves.

If I had to point to one single feature that makes this way of life possible, I would focus on *sharing*. Each !Kung is not an island unto himself or herself; each is part of a collective. It is a small, rudimentary collective, and at times a fragile one, but it is a collective nonetheless. What I mean is that the living group pools the resources that are brought into camp so that everyone receives an equitable share. The !Kung and people like them don't do this out of nobility of soul or because they are made of better stuff than we are. In fact, they often gripe about sharing. They do it because it works for them and it enhances their survival. Without this core of sharing, life for the !Kung would be harder and infinitely less pleasant (see Postscript).

[4] This point has been disputed by Wilmsen (1978). For a discussion, see Lee (1979): Chapter 15.

5/Kinship and social organization

One day in March 1964, I was visiting !Xabe village, when Hwan//a, a woman about my age who was married to one of Headman Isak's three sons playfully began to call to me, "Uncle, uncle, /Tontah, come see me."

Puzzled, I drew closer; until that time the !Kung had referred to me simply as the White Man (/Ton) or the bearded one, Tsikoie (Mandavo, in Herero). Hwan//a smiled and said, "You are all alone here and I have no children, so I will name you /Tontah after my tsu /Tontah who is dead, and, as I have named you, you shall call me mother."

Pleased, I asked Hwan//a to tell me how she decided on the name /Tontah. She explained that I was a European, a "/ton," and the traditional !Kung name /Tontah sounds like it. Since her late tsu had no namesake, she decided to name me /Tontah to do honor to him and to my exotic status.

It was hard for me to think of the young and attractive Hwan//a, not yet thirty, as my mother, but I was happy to have a name other than White Man.

This was the famous name relationship—the !Kung custom of naming everyone after an older person according to a repertoire of personal names. I had read about it in the writings of Lorna Marshall (1957), and I was excited to be named in this way.

The name stuck. Soon people all over the Dobe area were calling me /Tontah, and I began to sense some of the possibilities of the name relationship when a very beautiful woman, on whom I had a terrible crush, playfully said, "Your old name called me tsiu [wife], so I will call you mi!kwah, my husband."

But there was more to come. A few weeks later, back at the Dobe camp, I was sitting in the shade working on some notes when N!eishi, his son ≠Toma, the hunter, and his ex-wife, the redoubtable //Gumi, approached me with some ceremony and sat down.

"Mba," N!eishi began, calling me by the term "father," a not uncommon form of greeting, "Mba, we see that you are all alone here; your family is far away, and we too are all alone. We have no family. No one pays attention to us. So from now on I am your father, and //Gumi here is your mother, and ≠Toma is your older brother. From now on call me 'mba.'"

//Gumi broke in. "And you call me aiye." She used the vocative form for mother, the first word every !Kung infant learns, as with the English it is mama.

"And call me !ko!ko," added ≠Toma, using the vocative form for older brother.

With my limited !Kung, I signified my pleasure with the turn of events. Here was a whole family to be a part of, one with genealogical links throughout the Dobe area. It did not seem to bother anyone that I was named from one family and adopted into another. And with great cordiality people in the distant villages began to instruct me in what I was to call them.

But soon things got very complicated. My knowledge of the kinship terminology was minimal. A few people were calling me by kin terms that flowed from their genealogical connection to my own "parents," N!eishi and //Gumi. And a few others were using kin terms because they were related to other /Tontahs through the name relationship. But many others were using kin terms that made absolutely no sense to me, either as genealogical kin or namesake kin. It was clear that I had a lot to learn about the kinship system and social organization in general.

The process of discovery is the subject of this chapter. After describing the group structure of the !Kung, we will enter the fascinating world of !Kung kinship and its principal genius stroke: the name relationship.

The !Kung commonly live in camps that number from 10 to 30 individuals, but the composition of these camps changes from month to month and from day to day. In essence, a !Kung camp consists of relatives, friends, and in-laws who have found that they can live and work well together. Under this flexible principle, brothers may be united or divided; fathers and sons may live together or apart. Further, during his or her lifetime a !Kung may live at many waterholes with many different groups. Given their flexible lifestyle, and lacking a system of state organization as we know it, what principles *do* the !Kung rely on to give their life stability and coherence?

As in all other prestate societies, the central organizing principle of !Kung life is kinship. Kin terms are applied to everyone, related or not, and kin ties extend to the very borders of the known world. Kinship provides the structure of everyday life and enables the society to reproduce itself socially from generation to generation. But the multifold principles of kinship constitute, not an invariant code of laws written in stone, but instead a whole series of codes, consistent enough to provide structure but open enough to be flexible. I found the best way to look at !Kung kinship is as a game, full of ambiguity and nuance. The game of kinship has a serious side to it, but it is also fun, providing lifelong opportunities for deep play.

!KUNG LIVING GROUPS

The contemporary !Kung have two kinds of living groups. The first kind has a coherent internal structure, is usually fairly large (10 to 30 members), and is economically self-sufficient; most are based on hunting and gathering. The second kind is attached to Black cattle posts. These groups are usually units of one or two families whose menfolk work on the cattle; sometimes they are larger, composed of 30 or more individuals, and sometimes smaller—as small as a single !Kung woman married to a Herero man. I call the first kind of grouping a *camp*, a close translation of the !Kung term *chu/o* (literally, "the face of the huts"), and the second I call a *client group*, reflecting its dependent status in relation to the Blacks.

In 1968 there were 18 camps ranging in size from 4 to 34 people, and 16 client groups with a range of 1 to 44 people. The mean size of camps was 17.8; client groups were about half as large, with a mean size 8.6. In 1968 about 70 percent of the !Kung lived in camps and 30 percent in client groups. Camps were usually based on hunting and gathering, although several owned cattle and/or practiced agriculture. Client groups, by contrast, were always dependent on cattle herders for milk, meat, and grains.

The basic traditional !Kung living group is the camp, a noncorporate, bilaterally organized group of people who live in a single settlement and who move together for at least part of the year. The camp is a flexible but not a random assortment of individuals. At the center of each camp is a core of related older people—usually siblings or cousins—who are generally acknowledged the owners—*k"ausi*—of the waterhole. Around each waterhole is a bloc of land—the *n!ore*—which contains food resources and other waterpoints and which is the basic subsistence area for the resident group. The *k"ausi* are generally recognized as the "hosts" whom one approaches for permission when visiting at a waterhole. The *k"ausi* are simply the people who have lived at the waterhole longer than any others. They include both male and female kin and their spouses. The name of one member of the core group through time becomes associated with the camp as a whole, and the camp becomes known by that person's name. An example is *≠Toma//gwe chu/to* (*≠Toma//gwe's camp*) at Dobe.[1]

The *k"ausi* provide continuity with the past through an association with a waterhole that may extend over 50 years or more. Rarely, however, does this association go back as far as the grandparent generation of the oldest *k"ausi*. To put it another way, the half-life of a core group's tenure at a waterhole can be estimated at 30 to 50 years (Lee 1972b:129). A second integrative role for the *k"ausi* is the genealogical focus they provide. A camp is built up gradually through time by the addition of in-marrying spouses of the core siblings. These spouses in turn may bring in *their* siblings and their spouses, so that the basic genealogical structure of the camp assumes the form of a chain of spouses and siblings radiating from the core, as shown in Figure 5–1. At a given time the camp is composed largely of persons related by primary ties: almost every member has a parent, a child, a sibling, or a spouse to link him or her to the core.

Let us examine the process of group structure by looking at the evolution of a single camp, the Dobe camp (Figure 5–2). The core siblings, //Koka and her younger brother N!eishi, moved into Dobe around 1930. After the former owners died or moved away, they became the *k"ausi*. They brought in their spouses (3, 4, 5), and the children of these marriages (6, 7, 8, 9) later brought in their spouses

---

[1] This leader is *not* in any sense a headman. Lorna Marshall (1963:344ff) originally argued that ownership of each waterhole resided in the person of a band headman, who was always male and who inherited his position patrilineally. My research indicated that no headman existed either among the Dobe or the Nyae Nyae !Kung, and subsequently Marshall revised her view accordingly and retracted the headman concept (1976:191–195). (See also Chapter 7.)

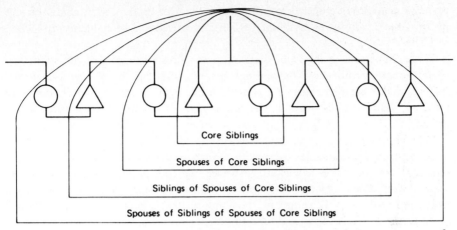

Figure 5–1. Groups are formed through chains of siblings and their spouses, and their siblings and their spouses.

(10, 11) to live at Dobe (segments 1 and 2). After N/ahka (11) had been married to /Xashe (6) for several years, her entire family joined her at Dobe, including her six brothers and sisters (13, 14, 15, 16, 17, 18), her parents (19, 20), her maternal grandfather (21), and her mother's brother (22). Later, when two of her siblings (17, 18) married, their spouses also came to Dobe (23, 24) (segment 3).

On the other side, in 1955, ≠Toma (9) married a 45-year-old widow, Tin!kai (12), who brought her adolescent son (25) to Dobe. Around 1960, the son mar-

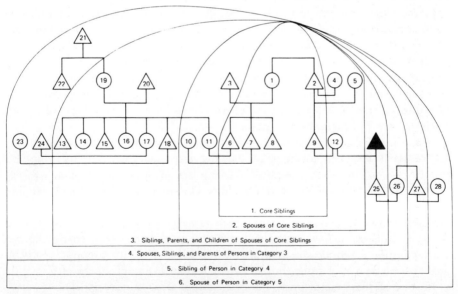

Figure 5–2. The evolution of the main Dobe camp to 1964.

ried a woman (26) who, in turn, brought her younger brother (27) along. Finally, in 1964, the last link was established when 27 married and brought his wife (28) to Dobe.

Of the 28 persons in the Dobe diagram, 6 are cores and another 6 are spouses of cores; 9 more members are the siblings, parents, and children of the in-marrying spouses; and 7 are more distantly related. All camp members, however, can trace their relation to the core through the primary ties of sibling, parents, offspring, or spouse.

Do core groups tend to be dominated by males or females? An older theory of band organization, traceable to Radcliffe-Brown (1930), put male siblings at the center of groups. In the Dobe case, however, the core group is composed of siblings of *both* sexes, and this is typical of the core groups in the Dobe area as a whole. An analysis of 12 camps in 1964 showed that a brother and sister formed the core in 4 cases, two sisters and one brother in 2 cases, and two brothers and one sister in 1 case. In addition, 4 camps had cores composed of two sisters, and one had a core composed of two brothers. These combinations are to be expected in a strongly bilateral society such as the !Kung, and the results serve to emphasize the futility of trying to establish whether the !Kung have matrilocal or patrilocal residence arrangements.

What makes camps change in numbers and composition? Short-term processes of three kinds set people in motion: exhaustion of local food resources, visiting and receiving visitors, and conflict within the group. In actual practice, it is often difficult to distinguish between each of these causes. When an argument breaks out in a camp, suddenly the food resources of another area become more attractive. The !Kung love to go visiting, and the practice acts as a safety valve when tempers get frayed. In fact, the !Kung usually move, not when their food is exhausted, but rather when only their patience is exhausted (see also Chapter 7).

In the longer run, processes that affect group composition include residential shifts at marriage, the adjustment of sex and dependency ratios, and the adjustment of overall numbers. In the first instance, the marriage of a boy to a girl usually results in the boy taking up residence in his in-laws' village. This practice, known as bride-service, is discussed in Chapter 6. But frequently the boy's brother or sister and their spouses may also join him for weeks or months, and occasionally his parents as well. Thus entire families may come together at the time of a marriage, and not just the bride and groom.

When a group's dependency ratio—the proportion of dependents per 100 able-bodied producers—gets too high or too low, steps may be taken to bring this ratio back into line. For example, if a camp has many young children to feed, this creates a burden on the working adults. One or more of the young families may be encouraged to hive off and join other camps where the dependency ratios are more favorable. Similarly, a group with few or no young children may see its future in jeopardy and take steps to recruit a related family with young children to take up the n!ore. By these means the reproduction of the groups is perpetuated and the burden of work effort is evenly allocated throughout the area.

In spite of these mechanisms, however, groups don't survive indefinitely. Each decade some disband and their members distribute themselves among their kin

Women and girls participating in a joking relationship.

in other camps. For example, of the 16 Dobe-area camps in 1964, 10 were intact in 1973, while 6 had disbanded, and 6 new camps had come into being.[2]

All this visiting, shifting, and adjusting of numbers will make sense to us when we realize that the !Kung camp is a unit of sharing. The food brought into a camp each day is distributed widely so that each member receives an equitable share. Thus, it is crucial that the people in the camp get along well together. If arguments break out, then sharing breaks down, and when that happens the basis for camp life is lost. Only when one or both of the feuding parties leave or when they settle their differences can the sharing be restored.

The dynamic of !Kung camp life is thus composed of work and leisure, harmony and conflict, and group solidarity interspersed with periods of group fission.

THE KINSHIP SYSTEM

We have said that kinship is the central organizing principle of societies like the !Kung. The purpose of this section is to spell out the particular features of the !Kung kinship system and to get you, the reader, inside the system so that you can see the world around you as the !Kung see it.

---

[2] I'm sure that a certain amount of group disbanding occurred in every decade, but I now believe that the groups were more stable in the past than they were in 1963–1973, a period leading up to major socioeconomic changes (see Chapters 9 and 10).

In order to do this we have to build up our kinship picture in three phases. We start with the kinship terminology as we usually think of it, a genealogical diagram with *ego* at the center and the terms she or he applies to all kin. We'll call this the normal kinship, or Kinship I. Next we will introduce !Kung personal names and the name relationship and show the rather different set of kin terms generated by this method, which we'll call Kinship II. As we look further into the name relationship a problem emerges between the rules of Kinship I and Kinship II: the latter seems to destroy the sense of the former. Just when you are beginning to despair, we introduce the key that resolves the contradiction and unlocks the secret of !Kung kinship. This key is the principle of *wi*, which I call Kinship III. As you grasp the inner meaning of the *wi* principle, a new sense of the beauty and coherence of !Kung kinship begins to emerge. Armed with that sense you will, I hope, be able to see the !Kung world as they themselves see it.[3]

Kinship I

Let us begin by introducing the kin terms for the immediate family. We will present the English-language equivalent first, then the anthropological short form, and then the !Kung kin term.[4]

	Short Form	Kin Term
Father	F	*ba*
Mother	M	*tai*
Son	S	*!ha*
Daughter	D	*≠hai*
Older Brother	OB	*!ko*
Older Sister	OZ	*!kwi*
Younger Brother	YB	*tsin*
Younger Sister	YZ	*tsin*

So far the kin terms follow our system, in that there are separate terms for F, M, S, and D, that is, F≠FB, M≠MZ, S≠BS, and so on. The !Kung differ from English usage in the kin terms for siblings. There are separate terms for OB (*!ko*), OZ (*!kwi*), and younger siblings of both sexes are lumped under the term *tsin*. Furthermore, sibling terms are different, as we shall see from cousin terms.

Let us consider next the terms used to apply to grandparents and grandchildren.

Father's father	FF	*!kun!a*
Mother's father	MF	
Father's mother	FM	*tun, mama*
Mother's mother	MM	
Son's son	SS	*!kuma*
Daughter's son	DS	
Son's daughter	SD	*tuma*
Daughter's daughter	DD	

---

[3] This presentation draws upon my own data and also the analyses of Marshall (1976) and Fabian (1965).

[4] We will be using English kinship terms, not because they always fit !Kung concepts (they don't) but as an aid to students' understanding.

The term *!kun!a* means literally "old name" and refers to the fact that male children are preferentially named after their grandfathers. The term *!kuma* means "small name" and is a reciprocal of *!kun!a*. The term *tun* for "grandmother" also has a reciprocal form, *tuma*, that is, granddaughter. These pairs highlight an important principle of !Kung kin terms: almost all of them have an older-younger reference depending on the relative age of the speaker. In a society like the !Kung, with few social statuses, relative age is one of the few status distinctions that can be made. Older-younger reciprocals are found in several other kin term pairs: *tsu–tsuma*, *//ga–//gama*, *tun!ga–tun!gama*.[5]

Next we consider the terms for the relationships we call in English aunt, uncle, cousin, niece and nephew. I will give you these terms now, but remember that these will have to be modified later when we introduce Kinship II, the name relationship.

Father's brother	FB	*tsu*
Mother's brother	MB	
Father's sister	FZ	*//ga*
Mother's sister	MZ	
Father's brother's son	FBS	
Mother's brother's son	MBS	*!kun!a or !kuma*
Father's sister's son	FZS	
Mother's sister's son	MZS	
Father's brother's daughter	FBD	
Mother's brother's daughter	MBD	*tun or tuma*
Father's sister's daughter	FZD	
Mother's sister's daughter	MZD	
Brother's son	BS	*tsuma*
Sister's son	ZS	
Brother's daughter	BD	*tsuma m.s.*
Sister's daughter	ZD	*//gama w.s.*

Careful study of these tables will reveal one important principle of !Kung kinship: the principle of alternating generations. For ego's *own* generation and for the *second* up *and* down, ego will generally use the *!kun!a–tun* pair of terms. But for the *first* generation up and down, ego will use the *tsu–//ga* pair of terms. To put it another way,

ego's own generation	
ego's grandparent's generation	are *!kun!a, tun*
ego's grandchildren's generation	
ego's parental generation	are *tsu, //ga*
ego's children's generation	

---

[5] The !Kung have a universalistic kinship system in that every single person in the society can be linked to every other by use of a kin term (see Alan Barnard 1976, 1978). The only exception to this rule, and the only nonkin term of address, is *≠dara*, meaning "equal". It is used for people of the same sex who are so close in age that an older-younger pair of terms can't be used. *≠dara* also means "friend."

Kumsan!a and his small name, Kumsama; they are in the !kun!a-!kuma relationship.

Following this principle, which pair of terms would ego use for great-grandparents and great-grandchildren? If you guessed *tsu–//ga*, you are correct.

The principle of alternating generations relates to another principle of kinship: joking and avoidance. All !Kung kin relations are either joking (*k"äi*, "to joke" or "to play") or avoidance (*kwa*, "to fear" or "respect"). And all of ego's kin fall into one or another of the two categories.

For a woman, here is how the kin universe is divided:

Joking Kin	Refers to	Avoidance Kin	Refers to
!kwi	OZ	*ba*	F
tsin (female)	YZ	*tai*	M
!kun!a	FF, MF	*!hai*	S
tun	FM, MM	*≠hai*	D
!kuma	SS, DS	*!ko*	OB
tuma	DS, DD	*tsin* (male)	YB
		tsu	FB, MB
		//ga	FZ, MZ

And for a man, the universe of kin divides as follows:

Joking Kin	Refers to	Avoidance Kin	Refers to
!ko	OB	*ba*	F
tsin (male)	YB	*tai*	M
!kun!a	FF, MF	*!ha*	S
tun	FM, MM	*≠hai*	D
!kuma	SS, DS	*!kwi*	OZ
tuma	SD, DD	*tsin* (female)	YZ
		tsu	FB, MB
		//ga	FZ, MZ

A person's behavior is very different toward joking kin compared with avoidance kin. With a joking relative one acts in a relaxed fashion and speaks on familiar terms. The fact that *!kun!a* and *tun* fall into this category highlights the affectionate relationship that exists between grandparents and grandchildren, a quality that is found in many cultures, including our own. But unlike our own, the !Kung take the kin terms for immediate relatives and extend them widely. The terms *!kun!a* and *tun* will be applied to dozens of people, and the feelings of affection are also widely extended. People in the *!kun!a–tun* category who are unrelated are not only treated with affection but, if they are of appropriate age, they may be prime candidates for marriage.

Toward an avoidance relative one must show respect and reserve, and one will often use the second person plural as a form of address (The !Kung make the same distinctions between familiar and formal that in French are represented by *tu* and *vous*.). The fact that one's parents (and children) and one's parents' siblings fall into the avoidance category is indicative of the authority that parents exercise over their children. People in the avoidance relation may *not* marry, even if they are unrelated. In extreme cases, such as mother-in-law/son-in-law avoidance (see below), the two parties in theory may not even speak directly but must use a third party as intermediary. Many of these relationships, however, can be warm and friendly as long as proper reserve is shown in public.

Among joking relatives, too, there is a considerable range of behavior. Towards your own grandparent you can be affectionate, but you may not engage in overt sexual joking. With an unrelated *!kun!a* or *tun* of the opposite sex you can engage in bawdy joking of the most overt kind, called *za* (see Chapter 7).

Finally, it is worth noting that the principle of alternate generations implies that if you avoid person "A" you will generally joke with his or her parents and children, and if you joke with person "A" chances are you will avoid his or her parents and children. All of a person's kin will fall into one or the other category. There are no neutrals.

These same principles apply to "affines," relations through marriage, which we now consider. The affinal terms are as follows:

AFFINAL TERMS:

	Short Form	Kin Term	Joking or Avoidance
Woman Speaking:			
Husband	H	*!kwa*	J
Husband's father	HF	*≠tum*	A
Husband's mother	HM	*/otsu*	A
Husband's brother	HB	*tun!ga*	J
Husband's sister	HZ	*/otsu*	A
Brother's wife	BW	*/otsu*	A
Sister's husband	ZH	*tun!ga*	J
Man Speaking:			
Wife	W	*tsiu*	J
Wife's father	WF	*≠tum*	A
Wife's mother	WM	*/otsu*	A
Wife's brother	WB	*tun!ga*	A

AFFINAL TERMS: (*Continued*)

	Short Form	Kin Term	Joking or Avoidance
Wife's sister	WZ	*tun*	J
Brother's wife	BW	*tun*	J
Sister's husband	ZH	*tun!ga*	A

Man or Woman Speaking:

	Short Form	Kin Term	Joking or Avoidance
Son's wife's father	SWF		
Daughter's husband's father	DHF	*n!unba*	J
Son's wife's mother	SWM		
Daughter's husband's father	DHF	*n!untai*	J

Note that the !Kung joke with spouses and with spouses' siblings of the same sex. This is because a man's wife's sister (or brother's wife) is herself a potential wife, and therefore a joking relation is allowed. The same holds true for a woman and her husband's brother or her sister's husband.[6] Relations between men and brothers-in-law and women and sisters-in-law, however, are tinged with respect. (An important variation is discussed in Chapter 9; see *Swara* and the *Sarwa*.)

The most heavily weighted avoidance relations obtain between a man and his mother-in-law and between a woman and her father-in-law. Here even direct speech communication is not supposed to occur. (In practice it frequently does, however.)

Summing up the presentation of !Kung kinship, so far one can see that it makes a logical, internally consistent whole. Kinship analysts classify the !Kung system as an "Eskimo" type of kinship, in that it has terms that separate the nuclear family from collateral relatives. Fathers are distinguished from father's brothers, mothers from mother's sisters, siblings from cousins, own children from nephews and nieces, and so on. If this system has a familiar ring, it's not surprising. American English kin terminology (and that of most European languages) is also of the Eskimo type. The !Kung make many of the same distinctions that we do.

But unlike American kinship, the !Kung kinship system makes extensive use of personal names in structuring kinship, and it is to names and naming that we now turn.

Kinship II: Names and the Name Relationship

Among the !Kung there are a very limited number of personal names in use. Only 36 men's names and 32 women's names were in use in the Dobe area in 1964. Names are inherited from ancestors according to a fairly strict set of rules. Every child must be named for somebody. A first-born son is supposed to be named after his father's father, and the first-born daughter after her father's mother. Second-born children are supposed to be named after the mother's father and mother's mother, and additional children are to be named after father's brothers and sisters and mother's brothers and sisters, in that order. More distantly related

---

[6] If a man dies his brother may inherit his wife; this practice is called the *levirate*. Similarly, if a woman dies her sister may inherit her husband, a practice called the *sororate*.

TABLE 5–1 MEN'S NAMES LISTED IN ORDER OF FREQUENCY.

Most Popular Names	Number of Men with That Name
1. ≠Toma	25
2. K''au	24
3. Kashe	15
4. /Ti!kay	15
5. /Twi	14
6. /Gau	14
7. /Tashe	12
8. Bo	11
9. Kan//a	11
10. Dam	9
11. !Xam	9
	168

Percentage of all men with 11 most popular names = 75%

Other Men's Names

— /Tishe	6
— N//au, N!eishi, ≠Gau	5 each
— Debe, Tsaa, Tsau, //Kau	3 each
— Hxome, N//u, /N!au, /Tontah (!), ≠Daun, !Xoma, //Koshe	2 each
— Ko/tun, Kum/to, N!ani, Tsama, /Tan!au, /Tuka, /Tushe, ≠N//au, !Kaha	1 each

n = 36

kin, and affines, may also provide names to a family. Parents may *never* name a child after themselves.

All !Kung names are sex-linked. A man and a woman may never have the same name. Further, the !Kung have no surnames. The result of this naming is that each man's name may be inherited and shared by up to 25 other men, and each woman's name by up to 25 women. Table 5–1 lists the 36 men's names in use in the Dobe area in 1964, and Table 5–2 lists the 32 women's names. It is interesting to note that 75 percent of all the men have one or another of the 11 most popular men's names, while 73 percent of all women have one of the most popular women's names.

Since the !Kung have no surnames, there is a real problem in sorting out one ≠Toma from another. The !Kung get around this by using nicknames extensively, usually highlighting, or spoofing, some characteristic or quirk of their owners: ≠Toma short, Bo tall, Debe big belly, N!ai short face (of John Marshall's film *N!ai*) are some examples. The leader of Dobe camp is ≠Toma //gwe—≠Toma sour plum, referring to his liking for the fruit but also nicely capturing his acidic personality. East of Dobe, many men and women have nicknames given to them by Herero and Tswana, such as Kasupe, Kashitambo, Kopela Maswe, and others.

What is the relation between people bearing the same name? If your name is ≠Toma, for example, you are likely to find about 25 other ≠Tomas in the population, all of whom claim descent from the same original ≠Toma and claim to be related to you. All ≠Tomas older than yourself you address as *!kun!a* (old name)

TABLE 5–2   WOMEN'S NAMES LISTED IN ORDER OF FREQUENCY.

Most Popular Names	Number of Women with That Name
1. N!uhka	26
2. Chu!ko	23
3. N≠tisa	19
4. /Twa	16
5. //Kushe	15
6. N/ahka	14
7. Di//kau	13
8. N!ai	13
9. Hwan//a	11
10. Karu	10
11. /Tasa	9
12. //Koka	8
	177

Percentage of all women with 12 most popular names = 73%

Other Women's Names	
— Bau, Sa//gai, Tin!kay, //N	7 each
— Chwa, /Toishe	6 each
— Kun//a	5
— Kwoba	4
— //Gau	3
— Be, Kxore, N//au, ≠Tabo	2 each
— !Ku, Kxamshe, /Tam, /Xia, //Kau!kobe, //Gumi, //Nsa	1 each

n = 32

and all ≠Tomas younger than yourselves you address as *!kuma* (young name), regardless of what your genealogical connection is and even if you have no discernible genealogical connection at all.

In reckoning kinship, the possession of a common name thus leapfrogs over the genealogical ties and creates close kinship even with distant relatives. Similarly, anyone with your father's name you call "father," anyone with your wife's name you may call "wife," anyone with your son's name you may call "son," and so on. And you will be called various kin terms by others according to what your name means to them.

The name relationship has an important bearing on marriage arrangements. A woman may not marry a man with her father's or brother's name, and a man may not marry a woman with his mother's or sister's name. Thus, for a man, if your mother has a common name and you have several sisters with common names, up to 50 percent of all the potential spouses may be off limits to you. For example, a man named ≠Toma will be ineligible as a spouse for the approximately 50 women with fathers or brothers named ≠Toma. And if his mother is a N!uhka and he has sisters named Chu!ko and N≠tisa, another 68 woman will be barred from marrying him.

The principle of the name relationship has a certain logic to it, and it is obviously of great benefit in tying society together by making close kin out of distant strangers. But is should be clear that it is a great *destroyer* of the logic of the standard kinship system we outlined on pages 62-66. In fact, the two systems are often completely at odds.

To illustrate, let us take the not infrequent case of a man who is named after his father's or mother's brother and not for his father's or mother's father.[7] His FB becomes his *!kun!a*, a joking term, and his FF becomes a *tsu*, an avoidance term. Now what about his FBS, who ordinarily would be a *!kuma*? He now must become a *tsuma* if the principle of alternating generations is to hold. In short, in up to half the cases ego will find himself out of step with Kinship I and out of step with his brothers and sisters, who will joke with those he avoids and who must avoid those he jokes with.

But the problem doesn't stop there. The name relationship also introduces complications into the marriage market. For instance, consider the case of a young man named ≠Toma who finds an attractive young woman named Chu/o. She happens to have the same name as his *tun*; this makes Chu/o not only a joking partner but also highly eligible as a spouse for ≠Toma. But wait! The attractive woman's father's name happens to be ≠Toma as well, and this makes our young ≠Toma strictly off limits *to her*. His name system makes her an eligible spouse; her name system makes him *verboten*. Whose view is to prevail? When such an impasse occurs, the !Kung say *sa ge a //kemi*—"they are in the middle"—that is, they are halfway between the joking and the avoidance categories. In such cases avoidance takes priority over joking, and a marriage is unlikely to occur.

Because so many !Kung share the same names, this sort of problem crops up again and again. Given these contradictions between the "normal" kinship of system I and system II generated by the name relationship, how can we go about finding out which system takes primacy, or at least how the two systems interlock?

Kinship III: The Principle of Wi

The method I first used to tackle this problem in the field was to interview many people and ask them to give me the kin terms they applied to each of up to thirty relatives. This task proved extremely time-consuming and frustrating. At first everything went smoothly with each informant: father was called *ba*, mother *tai*, older brother *!ko*, and so on, as they should be in Kinship I. Other kin were called *!kun!a* or *tun* if they had ego's grandfather's or grandmother's name, or *!ko* if they had ego's brother's name, as they should in Kinship II. But every informant had many kin whose terms of address *did not make sense either in terms of Kinship I or Kinship II*! Each older !Kung could rattle off terms for all his or her kin without hesitation, but when I asked why they used a particular term the answer made little sense to me.

I resolved that there must be some additional principle or principles that were escaping me. After months of muddle, the clue came when I asked the following question of old !Xam, a 70-year-old /Xai/xai man: "When two people are working out what kin term to employ, how do you decide whose choice is to prevail?"

---

[7] Lorna Marshall's data show that only 51 percent of the !Kung are named for grandparents (Marshall 1976:244).

"In our way," !Xam replied, "it is always the older person who '*wis*' the younger person. Since I am older than you, I decide what we should call each other."

I had heard this argument before but hadn't grasped its full significance. The !Kung concept of *wi* is an interesting one. I had understood it to mean "to help" or "to assist"; now I learned that it also had the sense of exercising authority. !Xam explained that relative age was very important in !Kung kinship. In a society with no chiefs or headmen or ranked statuses, relative age was one of the few bases for status distinctions. It was crucial in determining who should choose the kin terms to be used.

As I explored the concept of *wi* further, its full meaning began to dawn on me. In fact, its use constituted a third principle of !Kung kinship, on a par with Kinships I and II. The principle that elders chose kin terms for juniors, when combined with the name relationship, make kinship appear quirky and unpredictable. Yet these choices made perfect sense when you grasped *wi*'s inner meaning. Finally, after months of plodding along, I finally felt that I had cracked the code; this is what I wrote in my field notes in March 1969:

> *Wi* is the great rattler and destroyer of systems. Because for the first half of your life you have to take all your elders' various *wis* according to *their* lights, not yours.
>
> But then turning around [in midlife] you take these well-established *wis* and impose them on your juniors of various names in ways that have little meaning to them *just as your wis originally had little meaning to you!*
>
> Thus *wis* seemingly devoid of logic keep getting passed on and such neat rules as alternating generations from either Kinship I or Kinship II can never get going.
>
> Against this trend toward nonlogical *wis* there is the continuing refreshing of kinship with terms drawn from real parents, real siblings, real *!kun!as* and later, real spouses and real in-laws. These give the individual's personal *wi* system a semblance of order, especially with his or her juniors (Fieldnotes 21/3/69).

Armed with this new insight, I found that the seeming confusion surrounding !Kung kinship was replaced by clarity. As the smoke cleared I was able to further unravel the system.

First, learning the system is a lifelong affair. Your kin universe evolves as you grow. As you pass through marriage, the birth of your children, and later their marriages, you add new names and new twists to the application of kinship terms.[8] Take the simple fact of growing older. Since elders determine the kin term juniors apply to them when you are young, everyone is older than you, and you play an essentially passive role in the game of kinship.

For instance, if your name is /Gau and an older woman named N!uhka marries a /Gau, she will call you *mi !kwa*—husband—or *mi !kuma*—small name—and this term will stick even if you have no N!uhka's in your kindred, or if you do have a N!uhka to whom you would apply a different name.

---

[8] The kinship system is such a wonderfully complex affair that certain older people, usually women, become specialists in keeping track of how everyone is related to everyone else. I used to sit in amazement as Sa//gain!a rattled off names, terms, and rationales for dozens of kin pairs.

Now let's say that this N!uhka becomes a grandmother and a baby N!uhka is named after her. You will now apply the term *tsiuma*—small wife—or *!kuma*—small name—to the baby N!uhka!. The kin tie that originally had no logical basis gets perpetuated and, more importantly, *begins to develop a logic of its own*.

As you get older, more and more people are born after you, and for these juniors you are in the driver's seat; you may establish the appropriate term in light of your situation. The older you get, the more "control" you have over your kinship, until at the end of life you will have *wi*ed everybody in the kin universe. In fact, when I asked a very old !Kung man how old he was, he replied, "All the people who *wi*ed me are *kwara* (dead), and all who live I have *wi*ed [that is, I am the oldest person around]."

A second aspect of kinship and the life cycle is the changes that take place at marriage. When a man marries, new vistas of kinship immediately open up. If I marry a N≠isa, then:

1) all women named N≠isa could call me husband (*!kwa*);
2) all husbands of N≠isas could call me brother or co-husband (*!gwaba*);
3) all fathers and mothers of N≠isas could call me son-in-law (*≠um*);
4) all siblings of N≠isas could call me brother-in-law; and so on.

Whether any of these terms are actually used depends on what the older person wants to do, but kin terms flowing out of marriage names, because they are reciprocal, are among the most popular of the name-relation kin terms.

/TONTAH MEETS /TONTAH

Armed with my new knowledge, my new name, and my new kinship network, I plunged with enthusiasm into the world of !Kung kinship. Every day, new relationships were unfolded as people from distant waterholes explained their ties to me. Women named Hwan//a called me son, men named N!eishi did the same. Sa//gais and ≠Tomas called me brother. Because I was a new person and genealogically a child, young and old alike *wi*ed me. Soon I was engulfed in a dense network of kin-ties and obligations. In only one respect was I lacking kin-ties. My name, /Tontah, was a rare one, being shared with only two of the 250 men in the greater Dobe population (see Table 5-1). Thus encounters with my actual *!kun!as* were few and far between.

It wasn't until my second field trip that I really came to understand what having a namesake meant. I was visiting a group to the south of Dobe, and I was told that farther on there was a very large camp of San led by a man named /Tontah. He had heard about me, his namesake, from visitors from the north, and he was anxious to meet me. Would I come down and visit him? When we arrived at him camp at /Du/da, my *!kun!a* was standing by the road waiting to meet me. /Tontah was a tall, by !Kung standards, good-looking man in his forties with an open face framed by a short goatee. I liked him immediately. He greeted me with some ceremony and said, "Come, let us go to the camp to meet *our* people," placing a particular emphasis on the word *our*. He was living with his wife's family, so most of the people were his in-laws. In fact, they turned out to be *our* in-laws.

*Hwan//a, the wife
of /Tontah.*

"And here is *our* father-in-law and mother-in-law," he said, introducing me to an elderly smiling couple. "And here is our brother-in-law," pointing out a handsome young man whittling a spear. "And here is *our* wife, Hwan//a," said my *!kun!a*, presenting me to an absolutely stunning woman in her late thirties with almond eyes and a disconcertingly direct gaze. I noted that her name, "Hwan//a," was the same as that of my "mother." This put us into an ambiguous situation, intimate yet respectful at the same time.

"And here are our children," /Tontah continued, pointing out first a fourteen-year-old girl as striking as her mother, then an eight-year-old girl and a five-year-old boy.

Wanting to play my role as namesake to the hilt, I sat down to talk and said to the eight-year-old, "Daughter, I am thirsty, give me water to drink." In a twinkling an ostrich egg canteen was produced and a cup of passable water poured. Refreshed, I spent the afternoon talking with /Tontah about the other members of his large camp—actually three semicontiguous camps of over 100 people—and how *we* were related to them. At the end of our talk my *!kun!a* made a comment on !Kung kinship that has stuck in my mind:

"If your name is /Tontah," he said, "all /Tontahs are your *!kun!as*. All who /Tontahs birthed are your children. All who birthed /Tontahs are your parents, and all who married /Tontahs are your wives."

Which is more important to the !Kung, I wondered, the genealogical tie or the name relationship? It is difficult to answer this question, but one line of evidence may be useful. I was both given a name relationship and adopted into a !Kung family. Most of the other anthropologists and other scientists who have worked with the !Kung—about a dozen in number—have only been given namesakes, and that alone, the !Kung feel, is more than sufficient to plunge them into the kinship network. The strength of the name relationship and of the principle of kinship in general is illustrated by the experience of a British film crew from the BBC. Within an hour of arrival at Dobe in July 1980, the entire party had been given !Kung names and been "adopted" by their namesakes, who proceeded to call them by their !Kung names for the rest of their stay and who never even bothered to find out what their English names were.

6 / Marriage and sexuality

Hwan//a, a handsome young woman of 18, had just given birth to a beautiful baby after an affair with a young Herero man. The man would not marry Hwan//a, nor did Hwan//a's parents want him to. They wanted her to marry a !Kung, but who would take her now that she was a mother of another man's child? In 1964 the problem of "illegitimate" children was still relatively rare, since most girls were married before or soon after menarche (first menses).

Several years before, a !Kung man named Bo had approached Hwan//a's parents for her hand in marriage, but her father refused, having another suitor in mind. But when Hwan//a's affair with the Herero boy started, these other negotiations were dropped.

Three days after the baby was born, Bo's mother, Karu, and her husband !Kam, from a village 12 miles away, came to visit Hwan//a's parents with an interesting proposition.

"We want to ask you for Hwan//a for our son Bo," said Karu.

Hwan//a's father refused, saying, "My daughter was spoiled by the Herero. If you take her, you will get into arguments with her about the child. And I fear that you will not take care of the child properly because it is born Herero, not *zhu/twa*."

"We are not worried about that," Karu replied. "We want to take both the mother *and* the child, and we will take care of them just as well as you would yourself."

After further discussion and exchange of gifts, Hwan//a's parents agreed, and Hwan//a herself agreed, and she and her new baby accompanied Karu and !Kum back to their village. A new marriage was consummated and a new alliance forged between the two villages.

The marriage of Hwan//a and Bo illustrates several themes of !Kung marriage: the arrangements between the parents, the giving of gifts, and the generally flexible and humane attitude towards sexual indiscretion. The "unwed" mother Hwan//a was not stigmatized or cast out but instead welcomed with her child into the boy's family, even though he was not the father.

However, in other respects the case above is not typical of the way !Kung do things. The purpose of this chapter is to discuss the changing patterns of !Kung marriage and sexuality, and to show the central role each plays in !Kung politics and culture.

74

THE ARRANGEMENT OF MARRIAGES

Traditionally, the search for a marriage partner for a girl or boy usually begins soon after a child is born. All first marriages are arranged by the parents and may involve a decade of gift exchange before the children are actually wed. Typically, a boy's mother would approach a girl's mother and propose a marriage. If the girl's side was agreeable the betrothal would be sealed with the giving of *kamasi*— a kind of gift specifically exchanged between parents of prospective brides and grooms.

Girls or boys are strictly constrained in who they may or may not marry. In seeking a suitable spouse parents must pay particular attention to the kinship and name relationships of the prospects. There are both primary and secondary prohibitions. In addition to obvious incest taboos against marrying a father, brother, son, uncle, or nephew, a girl may not marry a first or second cousin.[1] Additionally, she may not marry a boy with her father's name or her brother's name, and a boy in turn may not marry someone with his mother's or sister's name. Secondary prohibitions refer to anyone standing in an avoidance kinship relation to ego, including the kin terms, *tsu, tsuma, //ga, //gama, !ko, tsin,* and so on (see Chapter 5).

The result is that when a boy's and a girl's prohibitions are all put together, up to three-quarters of all potential spouses may be excluded by reason of real kin ties or name relations. In practice, parents of girls tend to be very picky about who their daughters marry, and if a young man is unsuitable for any reason a kin or name prohibition can always be found to justify it.

A case in point is Tin!ay, a beautiful pubescent girl who was still unbetrothed in 1969 at the ripe old age of fifteen. When I presented her mother /Tasa with a list of eligible young men of suitable age, she cordially but firmly vetoed each one in turn.

"What about Kau?" I asked.

"No, he's her *tsu*; he has the same name as her father."

"What about Bo?"

"No, he is my //gama's child! We are too closely related."

"What about Kashe?"

"No, he has the same name as Tin!ay's brother. I won't have my 'child' as an in-law."

"What about Dam?"

"No, my own sister N!uhka birthed him."

"What about /Gau?"

"Isn't he betrothed to //Kushe?"

"What about Tsaa?" (He was married to Tin!ay's older sister N!uhka.)

"No, I refuse *!gwa* [plural marriage]. N!uhka must be the only one!"

In /Tasa's eyes no one would do for Tin!ay, and several years passed before she was finally married to one Samk"au, a man whose name relation to Tin!ay was one of the joking variety.

---

[1] The prohibition of cousins as spouses is a highly unusual aspect of !Kung marriages. Foraging peoples throughout the world actually *prefer* or *prescribe* a cousin as a spouse.

*A young woman nearing
the age of puberty
and marriage.*

In the !Kung mother's view of things, an ideal son-in-law is an unrelated man whose name relation to the girl is *!kun!a* (old name), the most cordial of joking relations. Whenever possible the husband is drawn from this pool of fictive kin, though other joking kin are also eligible.

Besides the proper kinship-name connection, the parents of a girl look for several other qualities in a son-in-law. He should be a good hunter, he should *not* have a reputation as a fighter, and he should come from a congenial family of people who like to do *hxaro*, the !Kung form of traditional exchange. The last criterion is tested before the marriage as the parents of the prospective bride and groom exchange a series of *kamasi* gifts to reinforce their relationship. If either side does not keep up the gift exchange, the deal may be called off and a new betrothal sought.

The first two criteria can only be satisfied by close observation of the young man for an extended period. Thus the preferred form of postmarital residence is uxori-local—the groom comes to live with the bride's family for a period of years and to hunt for them. Only after several children are born can he take his wife and family back to his own people. Frequently, after 8 to 10 years of bride service, the couple elects to stay with the wife's people. Hwan//a, in the case study at the start of the chapter, made the unusual move of going directly to her husband's family.

Traditionally, girls were married at ages 12 to 16, boys at 18 to 25. In certain regions such as southern Nyae Nyae, according to informants, the girls' age at marriage was even younger: 10, 9, or even 8 years of age! When combined with the practice of long nursing and late weaning, one might see the amazing situation, in the words of one informant, of "a girl going from her mother's breast to her husband's bed in one day."

The marked age difference between spouses was another important reason given for bride service: a girl of 12 or 14 was simply too young to leave her parents, therefore the husband had to "move in" with his in-laws.

By the 1960s and 1970s the age of marriage had increased somewhat. Marriage of the very young had ceased altogether—the youngest age of marriage we recorded for girls was 14—and the girls tended to marry between the ages of 15 and 18. Boys were further delayed in finding spouses, and their marriage age had increased to 22 to 30. The greater delay in marriage for boys compared to girls had an important social consequence. Because the husband was 7 to 15 years older at marriage than his wife, this had the effect of giving him a disproportionate influence over the marriage partnership. The wives, however, as we shall see, had ways of evening up the score.

THE MARRIAGE-BY-CAPTURE CEREMONY

The !Kung marriage ceremony involves the mock forcible carrying of the girl from her parents' hut to a specially built marriage hut, and the anointing of bride and groom with special oils and aromatic powders. Unlike our Western fairy tales in which the couple live happily ever after, !Kung marriages start on a stormy note and continue in that vein for weeks or months after. In fact, the "normal" !Kung marriage has many aspects of marriage-by-capture, an ancient and controversial form of marriage in which a groom steals a bride. Today, elements of this ancient custom appear in the marriage rituals of many societies.[2] In the case of the !Kung, the elements of marriage-by-capture present are not entirely ritual in nature. They express real conflict between husband and wife and between parents and children.

These themes are illustrated in this account of a marriage at /Xai/xai between //Kushe, a girl of 16, and a young man named ≠Toma who was living in the east. The informant is /Twa, the mother of //Kushe.[3]

> When ≠Toma comes from the east we will hold the [marriage] ceremony. First we will build a house for them to live in. Then ≠Toma will go and sit in the hut, while we "mothers" and "grandmothers" (*tunsi*) will go and bring //Kushe to him. She will be crying and crying and refusing and she will be kicking and screaming against us. With some girls it is necessary to carry them bodily to the hut on the back of one of the women. But all the while we are talking to her and saying, "This is the man we have given you to; he is not a stranger; he is our man and a good man; he won't hurt you, and we, your *tunsi*,

---

[2] Marriage-by-capture was a favorite subject of nineteenth-century anthropologists, who traced its occurrence throughout Europe and the world.

[3] Similar accounts of conflict at marriage are found in L. Marshall (1976), Shostak (1981, 1983), J. Marshall (1980), and Volkman (1983).

//Gumi, holding forth on the subject of marriage negotiations.

will be right here with you in the village." When we get her calmed down we will put her inside the hut and all sit around the fire talking. Then as everyone gets sleepy we leave her there with an older girl who will sleep beside her so that //Kushe will be in the middle with her girl friend on one side and her husband on the other.

The next morning we will wash and paint them. First we will wash them with a mixture of *mongongo* oil and the seeds of *tsama* melons. Then we will take both husband and wife and paint them head to toe with red ointment.

When I married my husband Tsau [/Twa continued] I didn't fight too hard, but I cried a lot when I was taken to sleep in his hut. When the elders went away I listened carefully for their sleeping. Then, when my husband fell asleep and I heard his breathing, I very very quietly sat up and eased my blanket away from his and stole away and slept by myself out in the bush.

In the morning the people came to Tsau's hut and asked, "Where is your wife?" He looked around and said, "I don't know where my wife has gone off to." Then they picked up my tracks and tracked me to where I was sitting out in the bush. They brought me back to my husband. They told me that this was the man they had given to me and that he wouldn't hurt me.

After that we just lived together all right. At first when we slept under the same blanket our bodies did not touch, but then after a while I slept at his front.

Other girls don't like their husbands and keep struggling away until the husbands give up on them and their parents take them back.

This apparent struggle at the time of marriage is partly customary, but another part of it reveals a genuine underlying conflict. All first marriages are arranged by parents, and the girls have little say in the matter. If the choice is unpopular, the girls will show their displeasure by kicking and screaming, a way of asserting their independent voice in decision making against the alliance of parents and potential husband. If they protest long and hard enough the marriage will be called off. The fact that close to half of all first marriages fail among the !Kung is eloquently testimony to the independence of !Kung women from both parents and husbands. In some cases girls have been known to attempt suicide rather than allow a marriage to be consummated. (We know of no successful suicide attempts, and in all cases the marriage was called off.) But even if the protests subside and the marriage takes root, the struggles of the bride during the ceremony serve notice that she is a force to be reckoned with within the marriage and within the family. Another function of the marriage-by-capture motif may have something to do with the relationship of violence and sexual arousal. A prize that is won after a struggle is always more appealing than one that is handed over on a platter. The arousal effect may work equally on both partners. The notion that only males are sexually aggressive may be a projection of our own Western biases on our concept of human nature in general (see below).

However, this level of conflict is not sustained indefinitely. After the initial stormy period !Kung couples usually settle down in a stable long-term relationship that may last twenty or thirty years or more, terminating in the death of one or another spouse. There is ample evidence that !Kung men and women develop deep bonds of affection, though it is not the !Kung custom to openly display it. Successful !Kung marriages are marked by joking and ease of interaction between the partners. Only about 10 percent of marriages that last five years or longer end in divorce. When divorce does occur, the initiative comes from the wife far more frequently than from the husband (L. Marshall 1976:286). !Kung divorces are characterized by a high degree of cordiality, at least compared with Western norms. Whatever the cause of their split, ex-husband and wife may continue to joke and may even live in adjacent huts with their new spouses. (My "mother" //Gumi and my "father" N!eishi lived this way.) Since there is no legal bond or bride price, divorce is a simple matter subject to mutual consent. The same, for that matter, is true of marriage. The !Kung have no system of legal checks and balances apart from their own goodwill and desire to live in harmony. Thus we have seen marriages, especially of older people, occurring without any ceremony at all. A couple simply takes up residence together, and the community acknowledges that they are married.

PLURAL MARRIAGE

In a sample of 131 married men in 1968, 122 (93 percent) were living monogamously, 7 (5 percent) were living polygamously (6 with 2 wives, 1 with 3), and 2 men (2 percent) were living in a polyandrous union, sharing 1 woman. These figures illustrate the point that the overwhelming majority of !Kung marriages are monogamous. Although polygamy is allowed and men desire it, it is the wives who in general oppose this form of union. Polyandry is even less common and is con-

≠Toma//gwe and his wives N!ai (left) and //Koka (right).

sidered an irregular union. When it ocurs it is usually between older people past childbearing age.

Polygyny (marriage of 1 man to 2 or more women) is uncommon. Of the 7 cases in our sample, only 4 were producing children. In 3 others the co-wife was an older woman in a secondary marriage. ≠Toma//gwe of Dobe had a long-standing marriage with //Koka that had produced 3 grown sons. When //Koka's younger sister N!ai was widowed at age 60, she became a co-wife, with //Koka, of ≠Toma//gwe. An example of a younger plural marriage is N//uwe, the San constable attached to Headman Isak's tribal court. N//uwe married 2 sisters. The older woman has borne him 5 children; the younger sister is infertile. But the 3-way marriage has lasted over 20 years. Three of the 7 cases were sororal polygyny, while in 4, the co-wives were unrelated.

When looking at the reasons why some men marry 2 women and most do not, an interesting correlation emerges. All 7 polygynous men are healers (see Chapter 8), and 5 of the 7 have reputations as being among the strongest and most effective healers in the Dobe area. The ability to heal is shared by about 45 percent of all !Kung men. Therefore, if the ability to heal is a sign of power among the !Kung, then taking 2 wives may be one of the very few status symbols associated with it. The wives of the strong healers express pride in their husbands' ability, and they are also among the strongest singers at the all-night healing dances.

Against the express desire of men to take a second wife stands the overwhelming opposition of their first wives. Many married man have started negotiations with prospective parents-in-law only to have their wives threaten to leave them if a second wife enters the union. Sexual jealousy pure and simple is the reason given for the wives' objections, and in most cases the husband's plans are dropped. This underlines again the point that women are a force to be reckoned with in !Kung society.

Given women's objections to the idea of co-wives, it may come as a surprise that those women who *are* in this type of marriage get along with each other very well! The co-wives, whether sisters or not, strive to maintain harmonious relations, cooperating in food gathering and child care. The three marriage partners sleep under the same blankets, and sexuality is carried on discreetly with each wife in turn.

The !Kung term for polygamy of either the two-wives *or* two-husbands variety is *!gwah*, and the kin term for co-wife is *!gwah di-* (literally, co-woman). This term is also used widely among unrelated but friendly women as a term of cordiality. For example, women whose husbands have the same name may call each other *!gwah di-*, as do women who were formerly married or betrothed to the same man. The term for co-husband is *!gwah ba* (literally, co-father), and a similar rule of cordiality prevails among men married to women of the same name. For example, when my then-wife Nancy Howell was adopted into the name system as N!uhka, her namesake's husband /Twi immediately began calling me his *!gwah ba* (co-husband), as did other men married to N!ukhas.

Despite this cordiality, sexual jealousy appears to be strong among the !Kung. Women apparently love to joke about co-wifery with other women as long as they don't have to become actual co-wives.

INTERGROUP ALLIANCE AND CONFLICT

In a society like the !Kung, with so little property to argue about, sexuality and marriage choices are two of the main foci both of social solidarity and of social conflict. When homicide occurs it is likely to have been triggered by an argument between men over a woman. Because of this, the negotiations over marriage have an undercurrent of danger to them. If a promise is broken, or two men feel they have a legitimate claim to the same women, a fight may break out, sometimes with fatal results (see Chapter 7).

It is the threat of violence that may account for the fact mentioned earlier that some !Kung girls were married *very* young, at age ten, nine, or even younger. A clue is given when we note that the area where the girls were married youngest—Nyae Nyae—was also an area that had a high incidence of blood feuds (see Lee 1979:387). Informants argued that the young age at marriage at Nyae Nyae was due to the desire of parents to have their daughters safely married *before* rivals could stake their claims, or before the girl was old enough to have an affair with one man after her parents had betrothed her to another. If a girl was married before she became sexually active, peace could be assured in the community.

Though conflict might erupt over a betrothal, it would be a mistake to exaggerate its importance. After the early stormy period, the great majority of !Kung marriages are established without stress, and the couples live in peace and harmony. In fact, marriage is one of the major forms of intergroup alliance among the !Kung. The marriage of a young couple creates an important bond between the two families and their camps. The kin terms *n!unba* and *n!untai* refer to child's spouse's father and child's spouse's mother respectively. (There are no equivalent terms in English, although there are in many other languages.) The in-laws collectively are known as *n!un k''ausi* (or /*twisi*). The *n!un* relationship between affines is very strong among the !Kung. If the two families live far apart they will likely exchange visits of a month's duration each year. The *n!unk''ausi* are usually strong partners in the *hxaro* network, exchanging gifts through their children over a period of years or decades. In some cases the entire family of the groom may take up co-residence with the family of the bride. An example of this was the family of N/ahka, who married /Xashe, ≠Toma//gwe's eldest son at Dobe. After finishing his bride service, /Xashe brought his wife back to Dobe to live. In 1963–1965 a large party of her kin came to live with her and her in-laws at Dobe, including her father, her mother, her married sister with her husband and two children, a married brother and his wife, four more unmarried siblings, her mother's brother, and her maternal grandfather—a total of fourteen people (Chapter 5, Figure 5–2).

To understand the true nature of marriage in societies like the !Kung, you have to see that marriage alliances form an important part of the !Kung system of social security. If one has good relations with in-laws at different waterholes, one will never go hungry. If wild food resources give out in your home territory, you can always go visit your in-laws. *This* is the secret of why !Kung marriages are so important to individual and group survival.

THE "MARRIAGE" OF /TONTAH

In the winter of my first year of fieldwork I was staying in the bush with /Xashe and N/ahka, and with her parents, Kasupe and /Tasa. One evening as we sat around the campfire telling hunting stories, /Xashe turned to me and asked,

"/Tontah, back in your *n!ore*, your parents, are they living or dead?"

"Living," I replied. "Why do you ask?"

"And your wife and children," he responded, sidestepping my question, "where are they?"

"I have no wife and no children. I'm still too young to marry."

The !Kung laughed at my response. With my beard and my obvious wealth, I certainly appeared to them as part of the marriageable age group.

"Well," /Xashe continued, "who have your parents betrothed you to?"

"No one! The girls have all refused me." Another stock answer, and good for a laugh. "But I do have a girl friend. And one of these days we might marry." This was true. My good friend Marie Kingston had lived in the Kalahari for several months, and they had met her.

Turning serious, /Xashe said, "/Tontah, a man like you, owning many things, can afford many wives, and even if you have a wife in your *n!ore* you should have a wife from this *n!ore*. I, /Xashe, as I am sitting here today, take my daughter //Koka and give her to you."

The people at the fire loudly indicated their approval of this move, while the object of this discussion, a perky four-year-old, averted her glance and cuddled in the arms of her mother.

I had heard about the practice of early betrothal among the !Kung, but this was ridiculous!

"But, but," I stammered, "by the time she is old enough to marry me she will have an old man for a husband."

"Not so," replied /Xashe. "She is young now, but it won't be long before she can marry you. Two, three rainy seasons at the most," he gestured, holding up his fingers, "and you will be together."

"And think of what it will be like," said N/ahka, the mother of the "bride" and my potential mother-in-law. "In the morning you are sleeping by your fire and your young wife is up and around drawing water, roasting nuts, and cooking food." All this N/ahka pantomimed with gusto. "Then you wake up and stretch, you have a nice cool drink of water and a wash-up, and then your breakfast is ready." The people nodded and murmured approvingly.

Now N/ahka was really warming to her subject. "Refreshed and well-fed, you are now ready to hunt. You test your arrows and choose the ones to take; you shoulder your quiver and you are off. All day long you criss-cross the country. Then you spy an animal, stalk carefully, and let fly. The animal is hit; you give chase; it's up, it's down; you finish it off with your spear and it's yours. You shoulder the load of meat and stagger home, hot and dusty. Your *tsiu* has a nice cold egg of water waiting for you. You drink and wash up, and then *sha*, and //*gxa*, and leafy greens are cooked and ready to eat. You drink, you eat, you butcher and cook the meat, and drink and eat again. Around the fire your wife spreads your blankets, and you lay down to a good night's sleep."

The group was chuckling and clucking in appreciation of our domestic bliss-to-be. But N/ahka pressed on. "*Mi ≠tum*," she said, using the kin term for son-in-law, that is how it will be. But first we must teach you how *zhu/twasi*—sons-in-law— behave. Some men hunt for their in-laws, but as you have no quiver there are other ways. You can give us things: clothes, blankets, shoes, beads, food, sugar, tea. All this will show us that you are a serious suitor."

The group was particularly pleased with this last bit. They knew that *kamasi*, the gifts that flow between prospective in-laws, circulate widely in the recipients' village, and so all stood to benefit from having me as a son-in-law.

It was my turn to speak. "*Mi ≠tum*," I said to /Xashe, "and *mi/totsu*," addressing N/ahka, "your words make my heart feel glad. I like you and I would like to be your ≠*um*. But I don't know what my family would say. I will write them and find out. In the meantime, let us do *kamasi*."

This answer seemed to satisfy people. N/ahka, beaming, turned to her daughter and said, "//Koka, greet your husband."

While her age-mates giggled, //Koka stared sullenly and stuck her tongue out at me.

SEXUALITY

The learning of sexual behavior begins for !Kung children at an early age. Parents and young children sleep under the same blanket, and parental sex is carried on discreetly while the children sleep. Older children run naked through the village until age seven or eight, and it is only when they reach their early teens that they are finally expected to cover up the genitals.

There is a natural and unselfconscious attitude toward sex on the part of the !Kung, and this attitude is imparted to the children. Sexual play is considered a normal part of childhood. N≠tisa, a 50-year-old !Kung woman from !Kangwa, was interviewed in depth by Marjorie Shostak about her life experiences. Here N≠tisa speaks about her first experiences of sex:

> When a child sleeps beside his mother, in front, and his father sleeps behind and makes love to her, the child watches. Perhaps this is the way the child learns. Because as his father lies with his mother, the child watches. The child is still senseless, is without intelligence, and he just watches.
>
> Then, when he and the other children are playing, if he is a little boy, he takes his younger sister and pretends to have sex with her. And as he grows, he lives in the bush and continues to play, now with other children, and they have sex with each other and play and play and play. They take food from the village and go back to the bush and continue their games. That's the way they grow up. . . .
>
> Some days I refused and remained in the village and just stayed with mother. Some days I went with them. Sometimes I refused to play, other times I agreed. The little boys entered the play huts where we were playing and then they lay down with us. My boyfriend came to see me and we lived like that and played. We would lie down and they would have sex with us.
>
> /Ti!kay taught it to me, and because of that I liked him. I really liked him! When we played, the other children said I should play with someone else, but I refused. I wanted /Ti!kay only. I said, "Me, I won't take a horrible man."
>
> They teased /Ti!kay. "Hey . . . /Ti!kay . . . you are the only one N≠isa likes. She refuses everyone else."
>
> He taught me about men. We played and played, and he grabbed me, and we played and played. Some days we built little huts, and he took me. We played every day. I used to think, "What is this thing that is so good? How come it is so good and I used to refuse it? The other children knew about it, and I had no sense. Now I know when you are a child, this is something you do. You teach it to yourself. (Shostak 1976:262–263)

From this account it will be clear that the concept of virginity can have no real meaning in the !Kung context. Most boys and girls will have had some experience of sexual intercourse by age fifteen. It is curious, therefore, that girls express so much fear and resistance toward their husbands at the time of marriage. As we noted on pages 77–79, !Kung girls struggle to avoid sexual intercourse with their husbands for weeks or months after the marriage. N≠tisa, too, resisted strenuously the advances of her husband, /Xashe, even tying a branch between her legs with leather to prevent her husband's penetration (Shostak, 1976:272–273). Finally, after many further struggles, N≠tisa's attitude began to change:

> We lived and lived and soon I started to like him. After that I was a grown person and said to myself, "Yes, without a doubt a man sleeps with you. I thought maybe he didn't."
> We lived on, and then I loved him and he loved me, and I kept on loving him. When he wanted me I didn't refuse, and he slept with me. I thought, "Why have I been so concerned about my genitals? They are after all not so important. So why was I refusing them?"
> I thought that and gave myself to him and gave and gave. I no longer refused. We lay with one another, and my breasts had grown very large. I had become a woman. (Shostak, 1976:274–275)

Marital sex after the excitement of the children's play groups is of necessity rather restrained. The presence of young children and the lack of privacy further inhibit sexual expression. The preferred position for intercourse is man-behind-woman-in-front, with the two lying on their sides as they face the sleeping fire.

Younger couples may vary this by going out gathering together and making love in daylight out in the *t'si*. Except for young infants, children are left behind on these expeditions. Interviews with informants suggested that the !Kung use a variety of sexual positions, including male superior, female superior, front and rear entry. The goal of sex for both partners is orgasm, and it is clear from informants that !Kung have a clear conception of female orgasm. Several women said they regularly experienced *tain*, the !Kung word for orgasm, the same word used to describe the indescribably delicious taste of wild honey.

A number of forms of sexual behavior that are common in our society are rare or absent among the !Kung: oral and anal sex, coitus interruptus, bondage, and sado-masochistic practices do not appear to be part of the !Kung repertoire. Similarly, rape seems to be extremely uncommon among the !Kung (Marshall 1976: 279).

Homosexuality is not common, but both gay and lesbian forms do occur. N≠tisa described a number of same-sex sexual experiences with childhood playmates (Shostak 1983:120). A few adult men and women have experimented with same-sex sexual partners, with male homosexuality being slightly the more common. Of the two women and six men reported to have had homosexual experiences, all were married, indicating that all were bisexual. !Kung nonparticipants in these activities expressed attitudes of curiosity and bemusement toward them rather than embarrassment or hostility.

The question of marital fidelity and extramarital affairs is one that has fascinated several observers, but the data are contradictory. In many !Kung marriages the partners are strictly faithful to one another, while in a large minority there is evidence of extramarital affairs. For example, at one waterhole with about 50 married couples between the ages of 20 and 50, we recorded 16 couples in which one or another was having an affair. Both husbands and wives take lovers; there is no double standard among the !Kung. In confiding to Marjorie Shostak (1981, 1983), !Kung women spoke warmly of their lovers and the rare and precious moments they spent with them. Both partners, however, had to be discreet. If an outraged husband or wife discovered the liaison, a major fight could break out. Women, if anything, expressed more sexual jealousy than men, and if they caught wind of an affair, they have been known to attack their rivals or their husbands, or both.

MALE AND FEMALE AMONG THE !KUNG

We have looked at marriage and sexuality and have found that they are sources of strength and cohesion in !Kung society, as well as sources of conflict, disharmony, and stress. On balance, though, the cohesive side predominates: male-female relations are not riven with stress and dissension, and most !Kung would be considered (by our standards at least) to be blessed with happy marriages and good sex lives. Now we have to ask the question, is this blessing achieved at the expense of women, who are subordinated to their husbands' interests? Or, conversely, is it the men who are subordinate to the interests of women? Let us review the evidence. Arranged marriages do put a young woman at a disadvantage as her parents and her husband make arrangements about her future. But the young woman can make her needs known by vetoing the marriage, an option not offered women in many tribal and peasant societies. During marriage both men and women work around the "home," with the men doing more subsistence work and tool-making and women doing more housework and child care. No evidence of exploitation here.

The marriage ceremony does act out a ritual of marriage-by-capture and, as we noted, it conceals a real source of generational and gender conflict beneath the surface. However, the many forms of sexual oppression that women experience in other societies, such as rape, wife battering, purdah, enforced chastity, and sexual double standards are absent in !Kung society. In their sexual life both men and women appear to enjoy sex and to seek and expect to achieve orgasm, and both may seek lovers outside a primary relationship. And both men and women experience sexual jealousy and may act out their anger on spouses or rivals. The evidence on balance supports neither of the two alternatives mentioned above. Rather, we see a picture of relative equality between the sexes, with no one having the upper hand. There is no support in the !Kung data for a view of women in "the state of nature" as oppressed or dominated by men or as subject to sexual exploitation at the hands of males.

7 / Conflict, politics, and exchange

The !Kung are a people without a state; they have no overriding authority to settle disputes, maintain order, and keep people in line. Whatever order there is has to come from the hearts and goodwill of the people themselves. This is no small task. The !Kung, like all of us, are subject to the emotions that afflict people who live in social groups: anger, jealousy, rage, greed, and envy, to mention a few.

Yet the !Kung manage to live in relative harmony with a few overt disruptions. How the !Kung and people like them can live as peacefully as they do has puzzled and mystified observers for decades. Understanding their methods of handling conflict is the purpose of this chapter.

First let us look at the !Kung system of ownership and leadership; then we will go on to look at conflict and violence, and, finally, at the mechanisms the !Kung have evolved to maintain peace.

OWNERSHIP AND LEADERSHIP

Groups of people, not individuals, own the land among the !Kung. Each waterhole is surrounded by an area of land with food and other resources that a group depends on. This territory, or n!ore, is owned by a group of related people who collectively are called the k"ausi (owners). It is these people to whom you must go for permission if you want to camp there. Under most circumstances this permission is rarely refused.

The !Kung regard the n!ore as their storehouse or larder, and if food runs out in one n!ore all people have a claim on the resources of several other n!ores. The principle of reciprocity specifies that if you pay a visit to my n!ore in one season, then I will pay you a visit in another. In this way, guest and host relations balance out in the long run. As a result, there is rarely any cause for conflict over land among the !Kung.

I was fascinated by the smooth way these permissions were granted, and I kept asking the !Kung to explain how the system worked. /Xashe, a 40-year-old /Xai/xai man and a superb hunter, explained it this way:

> /Xashe: When I want to hunt at ≠Toma/twe's n!ore I say, "My !kun!a, I would like to hunt on your ground." ≠Toma would reply, "My !kuma, I'm hungry too, tomorrow you hunt and we will eat together."

RBL: How would you split up the kill?

/Xashe: I would take a portion and give the rest of the animal to the *n!ore* owner. In my own *n!ore,* //Gum//geni, all others have to ask my siblings and me for permission. I have refused some people. For example, I once refused /Twi from Due. We lived together but we didn't get along. He was selfish to me. When he distributed the meat he would get mad and not give me any; so I refused him.

RBL: Are *n!ores* ever owned by one person?

/Xashe: Never, even if you are the oldest you always say this *n!ore* is your siblings.'

RBL: Is it only siblings who own it?

/Xashe: No, other family members can also own the *n!ore.* They don't ask us permission. They just tell us, "We are going to the *n!ore.*"

Every !Kung has rights to at least two *n!ores*, the father's and the mother's. Wherever a person is living will be the strongly held *n!ore*, and the other will be weakly held. With marriage a claim is also established to the spouse's *n!ore*, and in the course of visiting and of siblings' and children's marriages, other *n!ores* become part of your universe.

The Problem of the Headman

We have seen that mechanisms exist for owning and using the land, but how are the major decisions arrived at? How is order and harmony maintained without formal political institutions? Some early observers of the !Kung reported the existence of chiefs or headmen who held political power among the !Kung as a first among equals (Schapera 1930; Fourie 1928). Lorna Marshall in her earlier writings (1960) spoke of a !Kung headman in whom resided the ownership of the group's resources and who inherited his position patrilineally.

If a headman existed, I resolved to find him, and in 1964 I set out to do just that.

After reading Marshall's 1960 article and the earlier writings of others, I made widespread inquiries in the Dobe area to find out who was the headman or chief (//kaiha) at each waterhole. The answers people gave were almost entirely negative. The younger people did not know who, if anyone, was the headman, and the older people were obviously puzzled by the question. Some people offered a variety of names, but most answered that the only headman they knew of was Isak, the headman sent out by the Tswana chief. Finally I discussed the question with K"au, a senior /Xai/xai man originally from /Gam. "Before the Tswana came here," I asked, "did the San have chiefs?"

"No," he replied. "We had no one set apart like a chief; we all lived on the land."

"What about /Gaun!a? Was he a chief of /Xai/xai?" I asked, citing the name of a man the Herero had mentioned as a former San headman.

"That is not true," K"au responded. "They are mistaken. Because among the Blacks the chief's village is fixed; you come to him, speak, and go away. Others come, speak, and go. But with us San, we are here today, tomorrow over there, and the next day still elsewhere. How can we have a chief leading a life like that?"

"If the San have no chiefs," I asked, "then how did /Gaun!a come to be labeled as the chief here?"

"I can tell you that. /Gaun!a was living at /Twihaba Caves east of /Xai/xai when the Blacks came. They saw evidence of his many old campsites and so they called him '//kaiha.' But they named him something that no !Kung person recognizes.

"But even that is lies," the old man continued, "because /Gaun!a was not even the real owner of /Twihaba! His proper n!ore is N!umtsa, east of /Gam. /Twihaba properly belongs to the people of a ≠Toma whose descendants now live mostly in the east."

Other !Kung informants corroborated K''au's statements about the absence of a headman among themselves, but the most striking confirmation of the point came from a conversation with another K''au, a short, lively Dobe resident nicknamed Kasupe by the Herero, who had originally come from the Nyae Nyae area. In her detailed discussion of the headman, Marshall (1960:344–352) had used the /Gausha waterhole as a prime example. The headman of /Gausha, according to Marshall, was one Gao who "chose to renounce his headmanship and to live with his wife's people in [Dobe]. . . . However, should Gao change his plan and return to Band 1, the headmanship would automatically fall on him again, as he is the eldest son" (1960:350).

Marshall's Gao turned out to be none other than Kasupe, living at Dobe. When I asked him how it felt to be the absent headman of /Gausha, he expressed surprise, shock, disbelief, and then laughter. With a keen sense of the irony of the situation, Kasupe insisted that he was in no way the headman of /Gausha; the !Kung did not even have headmen. If they did, he, Kasupe, would be the headman of //Karu, not /Gausha, because the latter was his father's true n!ore. Finally, asked Kasupe, if he was such a headman how did it happen that he, the boss, was living in rags at Dobe, while underlings, like his brother and sisters were living in luxury at the South African settlement of Chum!kwe?

Kasupe's genuine surprise at being named the headman of /Gausha, along with the abundant corroborating evidence from other informants, convinced me that indeed the !Kung have no headmen. Years later, speaking with /Twi!gum, one of the owners of !Kangwa, I casually asked him whether the !Kung have headmen.

"Of course we have headmen!" he replied, to my surprise. "In fact, we are all headmen," he continued slyly. "Each one of us is headman over himself!"

It is clear that, as K''au suggests, the headman concept probably came into existence as a result of contact with the Blacks, who wanted to incorporate the !Kung into their hierarchical system, and not as a result of indigenous !Kung politics.

The !Kung living groups do have leaders who may develop considerable influence in group decisions. These leaders work in subtle ways; they are modest in demeanor and may never command but only suggest a course of action. There is no hereditary basis to their role, and as often as not they are outsiders—men who have married into a group of n!ore k''ausi (landowners). This absence of hereditary leadership works for the !Kung, but it is not always an unmixed blessing.

When fights do break out there is no one within !Kung society with the force of law behind him (or her) to separate the parties and reach a settlement. Both the strengths and shortcomings of the egalitarian society are illustrated in the following account.

A FIGHT ABOUT ADULTERY

N≠isa was a beautiful married woman in her early twenties with a reputation for jealousy. Following the birth of her daughter in late 1967, she became subject to bouts of depression. For weeks she was brooding and sullen, and finally, on a very cold clear night in late June 1968, as the Dobe people huddled around their fires, her anger boiled over. She started declaiming to the village at large that her husband had shamed her. Dirty women with long black labia (a grave insult) were screwing him. She knew who they were and was going to name names. The camp was in an uproar. She began shouting insults at several of the other young mothers in the village, accusing them in the most vulgar language of having relations with her husband. Amid heated denials from the other women and the group in general, N≠isa then shouted that she was so ashamed that she was going to throw herself into the fire. She stood up and dove into the flames, only to be caught by three other women, who leaped up to restrain her. Finally Kwoba, one of the accused women, could take it no longer. She rose from the other side of the fire and came over to N≠isa and slapped her hard on the face. N≠isa jumped up and started grappling with her as other women intervened to lift the now-screaming infants off the women's backs. In a few minutes the fighters were pulled part, but the shouting and recriminations continued. N≠isa's husband Kashe angrily denied the accusations, while the other men urged that Kashe give N≠isa a good thrashing for causing so much ruckus. The accused, Kwoba, repeated over and over, "*Au zhi! Au zhi!*" ("She lies, she lies"), and others said, "This girl is the jealous type. This isn't the first time this has happened."

The cooler-headed observers agreed that N≠isa's suspicions were unfounded. Kashe was a serious-minded husband and father and, unlike some of his age-mates, was *not* running after other women.

By midnight the Kalahari subfreezing night had brought the conversation to a halt. The next morning, N≠isa and Kashe left Dobe with their infant daughter for a three-day visit to another waterhole. In later weeks the couple continued to live in harmony without further incidents, and N≠isa tried to mend fences with the women she insulted, who in turn were quick to forgive her.

CONFLICT AND VIOLENCE

The fight betwen N≠isa and Kwoba was typical of the dozens of minor and major fights we witnessed or recorded in interviews.[1] Far from being harmless, the

---

[1] Eighty-one disputes were recorded in all, including 10 major arguments without blows, 34 involving fights without weapons, and 37 with weapons.

Two men fighting. The fight was broken up before the deadly weapons came out.

!Kung can be scrappy and violent, and the violence sometimes leads to fatal results. My research on the period 1920–1955 turned up 22 cases of homicide, and although homicide ceased between the mid-1950s and the mid-1970s, it has recently flared up alarmingly in the late 1970s (see Postscript).

Given the lack of property and the widespread practice of sharing, what is there to fight about? And given the lack of governmental structures, when fights do break out what prevents them from escalating out of control? We will try to answer these questions in the remainder of this chapter.

Four years before my arrival at Dobe, Elizabeth Marshall Thomas published *The Harmless People*, a book on the !Kung that portrayed them as likable and inoffensive people who posed no threat to their neighbors. The phrase "harmless people," which has since become famous, is Thomas's free translation of their term for themselves, *zhu/twasi*, meaning "true or genuine people" or "just folks."

I was attracted by the characterization of harmlessness and was disposed to believe it. It seemed to correspond to Rousseau's eighteenth-century characterization of the "noble savage," a view of "primitives" with which I was in sympathy at the time. But my early fieldwork interviews turned up pesky and oblique references to a !Kung past that was decidedly not "noble" and that was out of kilter with the harmless image. Informants would preface remarks about some past event with statements like, "It was the year of the big fight at /Xai/xai," or "the year I married was the year that /Gau killed Kashe," or "My child was born the year after the Nyae Nyae people killed So-and-so."

After first ignoring these signals as evidence at odds with my prior position, I soon reversed my field and decided to make a systematic study of conflict and violence. My reasoning was as follows: because a body of evidence contradicts my a priori belief is *precisely* the reason to investigate it. (This advice, given by Charles Darwin in the introduction to *The Origin of the Species* (1859), by the way, is good advice for all scholars to follow.) I systematically began inquiring about homicides and gradually, reluctantly, people began mentioning cases. In all, 22 cases of homicide came to light, and 15 other cases of nonfatal fights, most of which had happened 20 to 40 years before, but some as recently as 8 years before my arrival. But I also found that the !Kung had many mechanisms for controlling aggression and preventing serious fights from breaking out.

The !Kung distinguish three levels of conflict: talking, fighting, and deadly fighting. A talk is an argument that may involve threats and verbal abuse but no blows. A fight is an exchange of blows without the use of weapons. And a deadly fight is one in which the deadly weapons—poisoned arrows, spears, and clubs—come out. At each stage attempts are made to dampen the conflict and prevent it from escalating to the next level. It will be useful to look at each level in turn.

The !Kung are great talkers. They may be among the most talkative people in the world. Much of this talk verges on argument, often for its own sake. Improper meat distribution, improper *hxaro* gift exchange, and laziness or stinginess are the most frequent topics of dispute. The !Kung call these *horehore* or *obaoba*, meaning "yakity-yak," heated but good-natured conversations often punctuated by laughter. However, there is more to them than meets the eye. Simply because these arguments happen to be funny doesn't mean that they lack seriousness. In fact, they proceed along the knife-edge between laughter and danger.

When real anger replaces joking, a "talk" ($n \neq wa$) ensues—an outpouring of angry words delivered in a stylized staccato form. John Marshall's film "An Argument About a Marriage" is a good example of the $n \neq wa$ form. (See Film Guide).

The $n \neq wa$ may escalate further to become a very grave form of argument, involving sexual abuse or *za*. The *za* form occupies the ambiguous position of being both the highest form of affectionate joking in the "joking relationship" (Chapter 5) and the deadliest affront, leading directly to fighting. Male examples include the insult, "May death pull back your foreskin," and female forms include, "May death kill your vagina," and "long black labia." Hurling a *za* insult arouses intense feelings of anger or shame and may lead directly to a fight.

!Kung fights involve men and women in hand-to-hand combat while third parties attempt to break them up (or in some cases, egg them on). In 34 fights recorded, 11 involved men only, 8 were between women, and 15 were between men and women. Fights are of short duration, usually 2 to 5 minutes long, and involve wrestling and hitting at close quarters rather than fisticuffs. Fighters are quickly separated and forcibly held apart; this is followed by an eruption of excited talking and sometimes more blows. Serious as they appear at the time, anger quickly turns to laughter in !Kung fights. We have seen partisans joking with each other when only a few minutes before they were grappling. The joking bursts the bubble of tension and allows tempers to cool off and the healing process to begin. Frequently the parties to a dispute will separate and go away for a few days or weeks to sort out their feelings. Fission is an excellent form of conflict resolution, and people like the !Kung, with little investment in fixed property, find it easier to split up temporarily than stay locked together in a difficult argument. ≠Toma//gwe and his brother-in-law N!eishi have been coalescing and splitting for years. After an argument they might make separate camps for a few months, only to recombine in a single village the following season.

DEADLY COMBAT: !KUNG STYLE

Despite the resort to laughter and fission as means of defusing conflict, not all fights are easily resolved. In all fights efforts are made to keep men between the ages of 20 and 50 apart. These are the people who possess the deadly poisoned arrows and other weapons. The pronouncement "We are all men here and we can fight. Get me my arrows." crops up in several accounts of fights. If this level is reached the situation is out of control, and the point of real danger to life and limb has been reached.

The period of my fieldwork, 1963–1969, was a time of relative peace. However, before 1955, poisoned arrow fights occurred somewhere in the Dobe or Nyae Nyae regions on the average of once every two years. My persistent questions succeeded in turning up 22 cases of homicide and 15 woundings during the period 1920–1955 (Table 7-1).

Fights usually broke out between men over a woman and, once started, might degenerate into a general brawl, as in this case (K1), which took place in the 1930s. Two men, Debe and Bo, were fighting for the hand of a woman, Tisa. This is a composite account of two participants, Debe and Kashe, men now in their fifties. Debe reported:

> We were all living together at N≠wama. Bo started it by refusing me a wife. I wanted to marry Tisa, and her mother and father gave me permission, but Bo had already married Tisa's older sister and he wanted to take her as a second wife, so he refused me.
> There was a big argument, and fighting broke out. Bo yelled at my younger sister, "What is your brother doing marrying my wife? I'm going to kill you!" He shot an arrow at her and missed. Then Bo came up to me to kill me, but my father came to my aid. Then Samkau came to Bo's aid. Samkau shot at me but missed; my father speared Samkau in the chest under the armpit. Samkau's father, Gau, seeing his own son speared, came to his aid and fired a poisoned arrow into my father's thigh. I was shooting at Bo but missed him.

The narrative continues with the account of Kashe, the brother of Tisa:

> Then Debe's father, Hxome, stabbed at Gau with his spear. Gau put up his hand to protect himself and the spear went right through it. Samkau rushed at Hxome

TABLE 7–1   !KUNG HOMICIDE CASES 1920–1955.

Code No.	Situation
K1*	In a general brawl over a marital dispute, three men wound and kill another east of /Xai/xai (1930s).
K2*	By general agreement, the senior of the three killers in K1 is himself killed in retaliation (1930s).
K3	The notorious /Twi kills a man in a spear fight (/Du/da area, 1940).
K4	The notorious /Twi kills a second man, an event that later leads to the killing of /Twi himself (/Du/da area, 1940s).
K5	In the course of being fatally attacked, /Twi manages to kill a third man and wound a woman (/Du/da area, 1940s).
K6	The killer /Twi is ambushed and wounded and then killed by the collective action of a large number of people (/Du/da area, 1940s).
K7	In a sneak attack one man kills another over the latter's wife. Wife first runs away with the killer, but becomes frightened and returns alone (≠To//gana, 1940s).
K8	A young man kills his father's brother in a spear fight, the closest killer-victim kin connection in the sample (/Du/da area, 1930s).
K9	A man accuses another of adultery. In the ensuing fight, the accused adulterer is wounded, but succeeds in killing the husband (Bate, 1930s).
K10	In anger over her adultery, a man stabs and kills his wift with a poisoned arrow and flees the area (/Xai/xai, 1920s).
K11	≠Gau from Chum!kwe kills a /Gausha man with a spear to initiate a long sequence of feuding (Nyae Nyae area, 1930s).
K12	≠Gau's enemies attack him in retaliation, but ≠Gau kills a second man in the attempt (Nyae Nyae area, 1930s).
K13	A relative of ≠Gau's is killed in an earlier fight that is related to K11 and K12 (Nyae Nyae area, 1920s).
K14	≠Gau's enemies attack him a second time at a place called Zou/toma, and ≠Gau kills a third man; two others are killed the same day: K15, K16. (Nyae Nyae area, 1930s).
K15	The attackers kill a woman bystander of ≠Gau's group in the arrow fight at Zou/toma (1930s).
K16	The attackers fail to kill ≠Gau himself at Zou/toma, but they do kill another man of his group (1930s).
K17	A young man not of the /Gausha groups kills ≠Gau in a sneak attack, finally eliminating an unpopular man (1940s).
K18	The younger brother of ≠Gau is attacked by another man in an argument, but in the ensuing fight, the man's wife is killed. ≠Gau's brother goes to jail in South-West Africa for this crime (1950s).
K19	Returning home from jail, ≠Gau's younger brother is met on the road and killed by relatives of the victim in K18 (near South-West African farms, 1950s).
K20	A black settler was having an affair with a !Kung man's wife. Catching them in flagrante, the husband shoots and kills the adulterer. The killer is later jailed in Maun, Botswana (!Kubi, 1946).
K21	A young man kills an older man with a club in a general brawl. The killer is later jailed in Maun (1952).
K22	In a general brawl a young man and his father kill a /Xai/xai man. Later both are taken to jail in Maun (1955); the last case of !Kung homicide in the Dobe area.

* This case is discussed in detail in the text.

with his spear and tried to spear him in the ribs. At first the spear jammed, but then it went through.

In the meantime several side fights were going on. My older brother dodged several arrows and then shot Debe's sister in the shoulder blade (she lived). I dodged arrows by two men and then hit one of them in the foot with a poisoned arrow.

After being hit with a poisoned arrow in the thigh and speared in the ribs, Hxome fell down, mortally wounded. Half-sitting, half-lying down, he called for allies. "I'm finished, my arms are stilled. At least shoot one of them for me."

But no more shooting happened that day. We went away and came back the next morning to see Hxome writhing in his death throes. He had been given cuts to draw off the poison, but the poison was in too deep, and he died. We left N≠wama and all came back to /Xai/xai.

This case illustrates some general features of !Kung arrow fights. First, the protagonists are members of closely related living groups. A second point concerns the rapid escalation and drawing in of more participants and the unpredictable outcome. None of the four wounded were even principals in the original argument between Bo and Debe over the woman Tisa. Another general feature is that deadly fighting is almost exclusively a male occupation. All 25 of the killers in the 22 cases were male, as well as 19 of the 22 victims. Of the three female victims, only one was a principal in a conflict; the other two were unfortunate bystanders. This contrasts sharply with the high level (25 to 50 percent) of female homicide victims in most Western societies. It may reflect women's high status in !Kung society (see Chapter 6).

The main weapons used are poisoned arrows, employing the same lethal poison used to kill game. Since a 200-kilogram buck will die within 12 to 24 hours, one can imagine the effects on the body of a human weighing 50 kilograms. Even with prompt treatment, a person shot with a poisoned arrow has only a 50/50 chance of survival.

The popularity of the poisoned arrows puzzled me. Why, I wondered, didn't the men fight with unpoisoned arrows and thus reduce the risk of death? To this question, one informant offered an instructive response: "We shoot poisoned arrows," he said, "because our hearts are hot and we really want to kill somebody with them."

Because of the very nature of homicide, when one killing takes place it is hard not to follow it with another, in retaliation. Feuds, in fact, accounted for 15 of the 22 killings. In only 7 cases was a homicide not followed by another—and another. In one dramatic series 9 people were killed in Nyae Nyae in a series of related feuds over a twenty-year period (Lee 1979:390–391), and other feuds involved another 6 victims. The prevalence of feuds brings us back to our original question: Once the pandora's box of violence is opened, how is it possible for people to close it down again in the absence of the state or an overriding outside political authority?

The !Kung do have one method of last resort, a trump card, for bringing a string of homicides to an end. I listened with amazement to my informant Debe as he unfolded an incredible tale of passion and revenge. This is a continuation of the case discussed above.

After my father's murder, Debe, a man who was my *!kun!a* [older namesake] complained, "Now my namesake Debe has no father, but Samkau still has a father. Why is this?"

I said, "You are right. I am going to kill Bo, who started it all."

"No," Debe said, "Bo is just a youngster, but Gau is a senior man, a *n!ore* owner, and he is the one who has killed another *n!ore* owner, Hxome. I am going to kill *him* so that *n!ore* owners will be dead on both sides."

One evening Debe walked right into Gau's camp and without saying a word shot three arrows into Gau, one in the left shoulder, one in the forehead, and a third in the chest. Gau's people made no move to protect him. After the three arrows were shot, Gau still sat facing the attacker. Then Debe raised his spear as if to stab him. But Gau said, "You have hit me three times. Isn't that enough to kill me, that you want to stab me too?"

When Gau tried to dodge away from the spear, Gau's people came forward to disarm Debe of his spear. Having been so badly wounded, Gau died quickly, but made no further move to harm Debe. However, fearing more trouble, some of our people brought in the Tswana man Isak to mediate the dispute.

The only word to describe the events above is an execution. There is no other explanation for the fact that Gau's people made no move to aid him as Debe walked into camp and killed him. This was not an isolated case: a similar outcome ended the careers of three other men, all of whom had killed before.

In the most dramatic case on record, a man named /Twi had killed three other people, when the community, in a rare move of unanimity, ambushed and fatally wounded him in full daylight. As he lay dying, all the men fired at him with poisoned arrows until, in the words of one informant, "he looked like a porcupine." Then, after he was dead, all the women as well as the men approached his body and stabbed him with spears, symbolically sharing the responsibility for his death.

I find this image striking. It is as if for one brief moment, this egalitarian society constituted itself a state and took upon itself the powers of life and death. It is this collective will in embryo that later grew to become the form of society that we know today as the state.

THE END OF THE FIGHTING

In recent years the presence of outsiders—Tswana and Herero—has had an important modifying effect on the way the !Kung handle conflict. Since the appointment of Isak Utugile as headman at !Kangwa in 1948, !Kung have preferred to bring serious conflicts to him for adjudication rather than allow them to cross the threshold of violence. The *kgotla* "court" has proved extremely popular with the !Kung, and Tswana and Herero at other waterholes frequently act as informal mediators in !Kung disputes. Many speak of the bringing of the *molao* "law" to the district as a positive contribution of the Batswana. A number of the !Kung men have become knowledgeable in some of the finer points of Tswana customary law.

The reason for the court's popularity is not hard to find: it offers the !Kung a legal umbrella and relieves them of the heavy responsibility of resolving serious internal conflicts under the threat of retaliation. The court has also provided the

!Kung some protection against unfair treatment and land grabs at the hands of the Black settlers (see Chapter 9). On the other hand, the impact of outside law should not be overestimated. Two homicides occurred in the Dobe area after the headman's appointment, and in Nyae Nyae one offender was killed *after* he had been jailed by the South African authorities. Recently the !Kung homicide rate has flared up again at the South African-run settlement in Namibia (see Postscript).

HXARO EXCHANGE

Despite their occasional flare-ups of violence, the !Kung do manage to live in relative harmony. We have already touched upon some of the ways the !Kung limit violence: the use of talking and joking to avert a fight or limit its seriousness, and the use of group fission to separate parties in conflict. But the major means of maintaining and fostering amicable relations between groups is through gift-giving (see L. Marshall, 1976). The !Kung system of gift exchange called *hxaro* is a far-reaching and ingenious mechanism for circulating goods, lubricating social relations, and maintaining ecological balance. Polly Weissner, who has studied *hxaro* in detail, aptly calls it a mechanism for reducing risk.

Hxaro in its essentials is a delayed form of nonequivalent gift exchange: I give

/Xai/xai woman making ostrich eggshell bead necklaces for hxaro.

you something today, and you give me something in return six months or a year from now. What you return does not have to be of precisely equivalent value as long as things balance out in the long run. The !Kung make a sharp distinction between barter and *hxaro*. A barter exchange requires an immediate return of equivalent value. *Hxaro* requires neither. The key to understanding *hxaro* is that, unlike our system of economic value, which is primarily about the exchange of goods and services for money, the !Kung system is primarily about *social relations* and the goods themselves are of secondary importance.

The clue to this came to me when I was discussing *hxaro* with !Xoma, a wise and dynamic man in his forties, a leader of one of the Bate camps.

"*Hxaro*," said !Xoma, "is when I take a thing of value and give it to you. Later, much later, when you find some good thing, you give it back to me. When I find something good I will give it to you, and so we will pass the years together."

"How close or similar should my return thing be to the one you gave?" I asked !Xoma.

"We can be living close together or far apart," said !Xoma, apparently misunderstanding my question.

Rephrasing, I asked again, "If you gave me a big thing and I gave you a small thing, would that be all right?"

"Yes, it would be all right," replied !Xoma patiently.

"And if you gave me a small thing and I gave you a big thing?"

"That would be very good, if it is your heart," replied !Xoma.

I seemed to be getting nowhere. I tried another tack. "Let's say you gave me a spear and I gave you three strings of ostrich-shell beads, would that be all right?"

"Yes it would," replied !Xoma.

"What if I gave you two strings of beads?"

"Yes, that would be all right."

"One string?"

"Yes."

"What about four or five strings?" I was getting desperate.

!Xoma broke into a broad smile. "I see what your problem is! /Tontah, you don't understand our way. One string, five strings, any return would be all right. You see, we don't trade with things, we trade with people!"

Any two people, regardless of age or sex, may do *hxaro* together, but the most frequent partnerships radiate from the husband-wife relation. A typical pathway goes from mother to daughter, from daughter to husband, from husband to his father or mother, and beyond. In effect, the parents of a couple reinforce their relation by putting goods into circulation through their children. The gifts before marriage, called *kamasi* (see Chapter 6) set this pathway in motion, and the goods, of course, move in both directions. People also do *hxaro* with siblings and their spouses, with parents' siblings, and with more distant relatives.

Every item of !Kung material culture theoretically may be put into *hxaro*: *karosses*, dogs, pots, digging sticks, pipes, jewelry, and so on; but the most frequent *hxaro* items are ostrich-eggshell bead necklaces and other beadwork, made by women and traded by both men and women, and arrows, spears, and knives, made

A !Kubi woman lavishly adorned with hxaro *beadwork.*

by men and traded by both sexes. A particularly popular class of *hxaro* goods in recent years has been items of European origin, especially clothing: hats, shirts, pants, dresses, scarves, and shoes; and iron cooking pots, enamelware, and other utensils. Glass beads of European origin (most Czechoslovakian) are highly prized. Using beads of different colors, the women weave and sew intricately patterned headbands, which are a primary medium of *hxaro* exchange. The designs are named and are original to the !Kung; they constitute an indigenous !Kung art form. It is likely that European goods reached the Dobe area through long-distance *hxaro* networks long before the Europeans themselves arrived on the scene. The same was probably true for an even earlier period of goods of Bantu origin, such as pottery and iron knives, spears, axes, and arrowheads.

Two classes of things were not *hxaro*. Food was never *hxaro*ed, although it could be exchanged in other ways; and people were not objects of *hxaro*, not even in a joking or a metaphorical way. Such institutions as spouse exchange and marital exchanges existed and were thought of as forms of reciprocity, but they were part of a different symbolic system (see Chapters 5 and 6).

Hxaro goods could travel for very long distances. In fact, the !Kung would draw diagrams in the sand of what they called *n≠amasi*, the roads or pathways along which goods traveled. A valued item might travel 200 kilometers over the space of two years, and change hands five times; or it could take three years to travel 100 kilometers and change hands only twice. These kinds of data are of great interest to archeologists (see Wiessner 1977, 1982).

The !Kung love to go visiting, and when they do, *hxaro* exchanges always play a part. In fact, it is not clear if the visit is the excuse for the *hxaro* or the *hxaro* is the pretext for the visit. When a family arrives in a distant camp, first they greet and eat, then the next morning they do *hxaro*. Bags of goods are brought out and, one by one, handed over to individual partners with a phrase like "I take out this small thing to give you," or "I couldn't find a really good thing, I just brought you this." Care is usually taken to play down the value of the gift, even if it happens to be a nice one. Then, either at once or a day later, the return gifts are made. When I first saw items being exchanged, I assumed that the *hxaro* was a form of barter, but the !Kung were quick to point out that I was mistaken. I was witnessing the halves of *two different transactions*. The first giving was the return gift of the *last* exchange, and the second was the opening gift of the *next* exchange.

The delayed aspect of the exchange was crucial to the !Kung. As one man told me, "If you give me something and I give you something back, we are even, we are finished. In *hxaro* you are never finished. One or the other is always waiting to see what comes back."

Occasionally the !Kung had major gatherings, usually in winter, when up to 200 people from 8 or more camps would get together for a few weeks. Here the *hxaro* trading would be intense, as people who hadn't seen each other in years would complete transactions and initiate new ones. Old people described the excitement of these events, when dances involving 100 participants would go on for two nights and a day.

!Kung men bringing a dispute to the Tswana headman's court for ajudication.

Hxaro did not always go smoothly. If a gift did not come up to expectation, it could mean a *hxaro* partner was losing interest in maintaining the relationship and was allowing it to lapse. This was a major source of argument, but fights about *hxaro* were usually a symptom of an underlying conflict rather than a cause in themselves.

Hxaro partnerships could also lapse by mutual agreement. And this was common in later life. People from 30 to 60 were the most active in *hxaro*. As people grew older, they traveled less, and their *hxaro* networks shrank.

Apart from age differences, not all !Kung were equally active in *hxaro*. Some men and women had dozens of partners and were constantly on the go. Others maintained only a few close relations with whom they did *hxaro* regularly. I wondered whether the active *hxaro* partners were wealthier than the inactive ones. The !Kung do have a word for wealth, "//kai," and a term "//kaiha," which can be translated either as "rich man" or as "chief." Hanging inside the huts of some of the active *hxaro* people was a bag or bags full of beadwork, ironware, and other valuables. These the people called //kai—wealth.

I asked !Xoma, "What makes a man a //kaiha—if he has many bags of //kai in his hut?"

"Holding //kai does not make you a //kaiha," replied !Xoma. "It is when someone makes many goods travel around that we might call him //kaiha."

What !Xoma seemed to be saying was that it wasn't the number of your goods that constituted your wealth, it was the number of your friends. The wealthy person was measured by the frequency of his or her transactions and not by the inventory of goods on hand.

In fact, according to the logic of the !Kung system, display of wealth would simply result in people asking you to give them the visible items. In !Kung custom it is very difficult to say no to such requests.[2] Therefore, any accumulation of wealth would be quickly dissipated.

Leveling of wealth differences, therefore, is one of the key functions that *hxaro* serves in !Kung life. Another function has also been mentioned: the obtaining of exotic goods that are not available locally through long-distance *hxaro*.

Several other functions should also be mentioned. *Hxaro* relations give people an entrée into a number of different groups. Thus, in the event of local group conflict the parties may cool off by visiting other groups for the purpose of *hxaro*. This set of options is particularly important ecologically. As I pointed out in Chapter 4, the Kalahari has marked regional and annual variations in the density of plants and animals. A prized food may be rich in one area and completely absent in another. Or a local wild food crop might be abundant one year and scarce or absent the next. Given these conditions, it is essential that groups be able to adjust their numbers by moving to adjacent areas when things get rough. Kin ties maintained and reinforced by *hxaro* are the means by which the !Kung are able to move when necessary to preserve ecological balance. In Polly Weissner's words,

---

[2] The only way to say no to such requests is to say that you have already promised the item to another. The listeners will be observant that you keep your promise and will be quick to point it out if you don't.

hxaro is a mechanism for reducing risk by spreading it widely in the population (Wiessner 1977, 1982).

In all societies, conflict and fighting are always a possibility between groups. We have seen how the !Kung manage conflicts and, when they fail to manage, how conflicts escalate to dangerous and even fatal levels. *Hxaro* represents the other side of the coin: the long-term institutions for maintaining ties between the people, circulating useful goods, and spreading the risk of ecological disaster so that everyone may live with an adequate, if not luxurious, food supply.

8/Coping with life: religion, world view, and healing

In previous chapters we have seen how the !Kung manage to make a living from their semidesert environment, and how they organize their groups, arrange marriages, and deal with conflict. But like all people, the !Kung live in a world of uncertainty, inhabited by forces beyond their control. Like all people they must face illness, misfortune, and the ultimate loss—death. Like others, the !Kung seek to counteract these forces and gain what control they can over their lives. Death is inevitable. But the meaning people attach to death, its causes and aftermath, is culturally given. Without meaning, without culture making sense of things, life would be impossible.

The system developed by the !Kung to make sense of their world involves forces beyond the natural order. Their universe is inhabited by a high god, a lesser god, and a host of minor animal spirits that bring luck and misfortune, success and failure. But the main actors in this world are the //gangwasi, the ghosts of recently deceased !Kung. The //gangwasi, not long before the beloved parents, kin, and friends of the living, hover near the !Kung villages, and when serious illness or misfortune strikes, it is almost always the //gangwasi who cause it.

The !Kung are far from defenseless in the face of these malevolent spirits. They have many spells, herbs, magic formulas, and practices for restoring health or good fortune. And if these fail, the !Kung have the powerful tool of n/um, the spiritual medicine or energy given by god to men and women. Armed with n/um, specially trained healers are able to enter trances and heal the sick. They go to the //gangwasi and cajole, plead, argue, and, if necessary, do battle with them to make them give up their grip and leave the living in peace.

The healing trances take place at all-night dances, the major ritual focus of the !Kung in the 1960s. There are both men's and women's dances, and new manifestations of n/um with new rituals are constantly appearing as young healers experience revelations during dreams, trances, or illness.

Though deeply immersed in their own world view, the !Kung are pragmatic about other belief systems, or as they put it, about other forms of n/um. They are interested in and fearful of the witchcraft practices of their African neighbors. And they take a similar view of the disease theories and treatments brought by the Europeans. They may seek out both kinds of medicine when circumstances warrant it.

In this chapter we will begin by sketching out their world view and their theory

103

of misfortune. We will then go on to look at two medicine dances in detail: the men's Giraffe dance and the women's Drum dance. Finally, we will look at the way !Kung beliefs are attempting to accommodate the ideas and practices of the Blacks and the Whites.[1]

THE WORLD OF THE //GANGWASI

My introduction to the //gangwasi came in the winter of 1964. In early July I returned to Dobe after a month's absence to find that misfortune had befallen the people. Entering the village I found Kasupe, the popular Dobe man whose relatives had figured prominently in the Marshall studies, lying in front of his hut surrounded by people. A curing ceremony was in progress even though it was the middle of the afternoon. While Kasupe lay prostrate a small group of women sang and a healer worked over him, rubbing his body with sweat and moaning in a rising crescendo punctuated by sharp, high-pitched cries.

From his wife I pieced together what had happened to Kasupe. While out hunting two weeks before he shot at and wounded a small duiker. Giving chase, he ran right into a steel trap set by the Herero for a lion. The jaws closed and tore deeply into his ankle. The pain must have been excruciating. Summoning all his strength, he pried open the jaws of the trap and freed his leg. Bleeding profusely, he staggered back to Dobe and collapsed.

I examined the wound. It was badly infected, wrapped with pieces of rag caked with dirt and blood. Fortunately, no bone seemed to be broken. The healer paused to rest while I peeled off the makeshift bandages, washed the wound, and applied a fresh dressing.

As I sat with him, he seemed to be resting peacefully, and some of the color started to come back into his face. I returned to my camp to unpack.

An hour later, ≠Toma//gwe burst into my hut crying, "/Tontah, come quickly, Kasupe is dying!"

I leapt up and followed ≠Toma//gwe at a dogtrot. Entering the camp, I saw a dramatic scene. Kasupe lay unconscious, totally drained of color, while his wife sobbed and his young children wailed. N!eishi was already entering into a trance and working on Kasupe, rubbing him, moaning and screaming. ≠Toma//gwe soon followed him, and the two old men worked over Kasupe for an hour, pulling out imaginary substances from his body and casting them away, standing up and going to the edge of the camp and speaking to themselves, and talking rapidly to each other in fragments of sentences that I could not understand. When Kasupe started to moan they redoubled their efforts until the air was pierced with shrieks and gurgles. Kasupe seemed to be breathing easier when they finished, but he was still a very sick man.

What had caused the relapse? And what were we to do with Kasupe? The nearest hospital was over 200 miles away. That evening N!eishi, ≠Toma//gwe, and I sat down to discuss the possibilities.

[1] Some of these topics are also discussed in Katz (1982), Lee (1967), Marshall (1962, 1969), and Woodburn (1982).

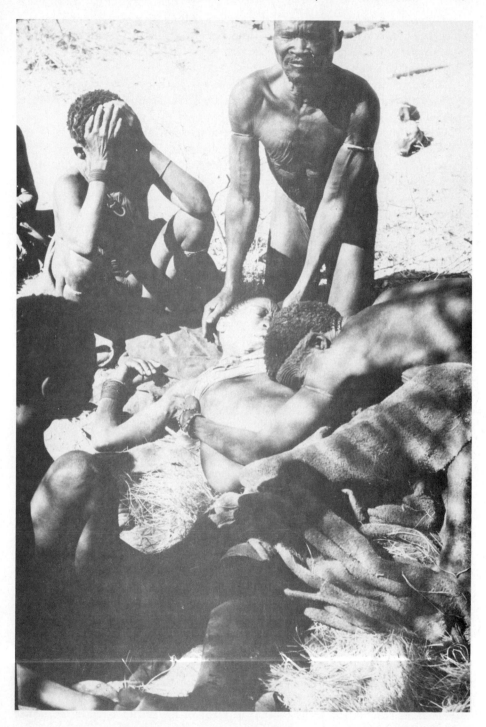

N!eishi and ≠Toma//gwe treating Kasupe on the day of the crisis.

≠Toma//gwe began. "It is not the leg that is killing Kasupe. I'm not sure, but when I was working on Kasupe I saw dead N≠tisa. If not her, then another dead one is trying to kill him."

"How did you see her?" I asked.

"When we are *!kia* [in the trance state] we always change into something else. We can see things ordinary people can't. Today I saw dead N≠tisa near Kasupe with an angry face."

"How do you mean, you 'change into something else'?" I asked.

"Your mind goes blank. You don't feel any pain. The ground seems to be spinning. We are different, a little bit like a ghost ourselves. And if the dead are there we can see them. We call them the *//gangwasi.*"

"Why is it that the dead come back to bother people?" That seemed the next logical question.

"I don't know why N≠tisa is bothering Kasupe. When she was alive she was just a normal person, on good terms with Kasupe. But all the dead were good when they were alive. It is when they die that they turn bad.

"Sometimes God himself kills people; sometimes it is the *//gangwasi,*" ≠Toma //gwe continued. "All we can do is try to cure the sick ones. If we fail, then we know that the *//gangwasi* were too strong for us."

I wanted to ask more questions, but I also wanted to get to the matter at hand. "What do you think of Kasupe's chances?"

"We don't know," ≠Toma//gwe replied. "We try to chase N≠tisa away, but she just comes back again. We chase her here and she reappears elsewhere."

N!eishi added, "Someone should go to Chum!we to fetch Kasupe's relatives. There are many big healers there among his kin, and it's important that they see him dying and take charge of him. If he dies with us, then his people might blame us."

I replied, "I don't know about *//gangwasi.* I only know that leg wound shouldn't kill a man. I can fix the leg with my medicines, but you will have to handle the *//gangwasi.*"

Both sets of healers did their jobs well. The next day Kasupe sat up and asked for food. The healers saw no signs of N≠tisa, and his leg began to heal. Three months later he was hunting again, and he was still living 16 years after (well into his sixties).

What had healed Kasupe? I'm sure it wasn't the penicillin alone. Equally important was the fact that his family and campmates had stuck by him and the healers of the camp had protected his life with their healing energy.

High God—Low God

The !Kung have not one origin myth but several. In one version, in the beginning people and animals were not distinct but all lived together in a single village led by the elephant—K''au and his wife Chu!ko. A large body of myths revolve around the cast of characters inhabiting this village, including jackal, dung beetle, python, kori bustard, and many others.[2] In many of the stories a central character

[2] Biesele (1976) has made a major collection and analysis of !Kung myths.

is the praying mantis, a trickster god who is always getting into scrapes and who usually gets caught and punished. The fact that the !Kung word for mantis is //gangwa has led some observers to conclude mistakenly that the San worship the mantis. In fact, the heavenly //gangwa is only remotely connected to the mantis.

The !Kung have two major deities, a high god called //gangwan!an!a (big big god) and by other names, who is sometimes connected with the elephant K"au in the myths, and //gangwa matse (small //gangwa), the trickster god. The !Kung volunteered the information that the English word for small //gangwa was Satan." How they made that connection, I do not know.[3]

There are varying opinions about the nature of these two deities. In some myths, the high god is portrayed as good and the lesser god as evil. In others the roles are reversed. Some !Kung regard big //Gangwa as a creator, remote and inaccessible, and see small //Gangwa as the destroyer, the main source of death. Other !Kung insist that it is the high god who is both the creator and the killer. Whatever its ultimate source, the !Kung do agree that the main agency that brings misfortune is the //gangwasi, the spirits of the dead.[4] Not all deaths are caused by the //gangwasi. If someone has lived a long life and died peacefully, they may simply say, "n/a m a"—heaven ate her or him. But in most serious illness or accidents, //gangwasi are involved.

The healers in trance see the //gangwasi in a variety of forms. To some they look like real people. Yoy can touch them and feel their flesh. To others, they appear like smoke, transparent and ephemeral. One healer described them as having only one leg, standing in midair. Some //gangwasi speak to the healers and give details of why they are there; most remain silent.

How Ancestors Become Enemies

What drives the dead to injure the living? This is a question I asked many !Kung. Some said they didn't know why; others said it was in the nature of the //gangwasi to do so. There were a number of ways of propitiating the dead so that their spirits would not come back. Ensuring that they have a namesake in the name-relationship (Chapter 5) is one such method, but it doesn't always work. Even spirits with namesakes have been known to bother the living.

For whatever reasons, not all //gangwasi are equally malevolent. Some never come back to make trouble, while others are major sources of misfortune. In a similar vein, some people during life led successful lives relatively free of care, while the lives of others were filled with suffering and misfortune. The !Kung themselves were not sure why this was so. There seemed to be conflicting opinions on the question. For example, a man named Kumsa≠dwin first argued that //gangwasi don't bother those who behave themselves, but later he reversed himself.

"We don't see the //gangwasi," Kumsa said, "but we know that they expect certain behavior of us. We must eat so, and act so. When you are quarrelsome and unpleasant to other people, and people are angry with you, the //gangwasi see

[3] There are many puzzling aspects of the High God/Low God dichotomy. In some myths there is only one god, leading me to wonder if the split isn't of recent origin.
[4] For a discussion of this question, see Marshall (1962, 1969) and Katz (1982:34–57).

A healing dance at sunrise.

this and come to kill you. The //*gangwasi* can judge who is right and who is wrong.

"But," Kumsa continued, "although //*gangwasi* watch over people, we feel that people should try to settle their differences among themselves. Because sometimes the //*gangwasi* try to pick fights among people."

"Doesn't this contradict what you were saying earlier, that the //*gangwasi don't* like people who fight?" I asked Kumsa.

Kumsa replied, "No, we have one story. The //*gangwasi* don't like us to fight, but they also make us fight.

"You see," he continued, "people have different types of //*gangwasi*. One may have bad //*gangwasi*, another may have good //*gangwasi*. People want good //*gangwasi* so you wake up in the morning and your heart wants to kill meat. Your //*gangwa* will help you in hunting.

"But you have no choice in your //*gangwasi*. You can't control them but must accept what they give you."

As Kumsa finished speaking, one of the listeners was visibly sceptical. "I don't know about these questions of good //*gangwasi* and bad //*gangwasi*, and not being able to control them. All I know is if I want something of my //*gangwasi* I just ask for it."

It is not surprising that the !Kung hold seemingly contradictory views on these matters. The sources of good and evil and of luck and misfortune have been a topic of speculation of every major world religion. And the answers they give have not been conspicuously more successful than those of the !Kung in unraveling the ultimate mysteries of life and fate.

The best answer I received on the question of why the living bother the dead came from Chu!ko, a vigorous woman in her sixties and an experienced healer. "Longing," she said, "longing for the living is what drives the dead to make people sick. When they go on the road that leads to the village of the //gangwasi they are very, very sad. Even though they will have food and company and everything they need there, they are not content. They miss their people on earth. And so they come back to us. They hover near the villages and put sickness into people, saying, 'Come, come here to me.' "

Chu!ko's answer made sense to me. She also spoke from experience. Recently widowed after forty years of marriage, she had nursed her ailing husband for months, going into small trances almost nightly and pleading with the //gangwasi to spare him. Chu!ko's view corroborated by others, made the process of death a struggle between two loving sets of relatives, one living and the other dead, each wanting the individual for themselves. The dying and those who survived them could take comfort from the sense that, whatever the outcome, the person would be in the bosom of loving kin.

Whatever the nature of their gods and ghosts, the !Kung do not spend their time in philosophical discourse in the abstract (except when anthropologists prod them). They are more concerned with the concrete matters of life and death, health and illness in their daily lives, and at this level they have evolved an extraordinarily effective method of social healing based on the principle of *n/um*.

N/UM AND THE GIRAFFE DANCE

N/um[5] is a substance that lies in the pit of the stomach of men and women who are *n/um k''ausi*—medicine owners—and becomes active during a healing dance. The !Kung believe that the movements of the dancers heat the *n/um* up, and when it boils it rises up the spinal cord and explodes in the brain. The *n/um k''au* then feels enormous power and energy coursing through his or her body. The legs tremble, the chest is heaving, the throat is dry. And strange visions flood the healer's senses.

As one healer put it,

N/um is put into the body through the backbone. It boils in my belly and boils up to my head like beer. When the women start singing and I start dancing, at first I feel quite all right. Then in the middle, the medicine begins to rise from my stomach. After that I see all the people like very small birds, the whole place will be spinning around, and that is why we run around. The trees will be circling also. You feel your blood become very hot, just like blood boiling on a fire, and then you start healing.

After a period of disorientation, the healer begins to move unsteadily toward the dance fire. He or she lays trembling hands on the chest and back of a person

---

[5] The *n/um* of the healing dance is just one of many forms of *n/um*. The word has a wide range of meanings for the !Kung. *N/um* can mean medicine, energy, power, special skill, or anything out of the ordinary. Menstrual blood, African sorcery, herbal remedies, a vapor trail of a jet plane, tape recorders, and traveling in a truck at high speeds are just a few of the contexts in which the word *n/um* is used.

and begins a series of moaning lamentations punctuated by loud shrieks the !Kung call *kow-he-dile*. She or he then moves to the next person and the next, repeating the action until everyone in attendance, men, women, and children, have received supernatural protection. If sick people are present at the dance, the *n/um k''ausi* will pay special attention to them, spending up to an hour working on one person, rubbing back, chest, forehead, legs, and arms with magical sweat. With the very ill, teams of up to six healers work in relays on several parts of the body at once. It is during these trances that the */ /gangwasi* appear to the people.

In addition to their ability to see the dead, the !Kung healers have other healing skills. They are able to put *n/um* into the bodies of sick people and novice healers in the form of sweat. They can pull (*≠twe*) sickness out of the bodies. Like shamans elsewhere in the world, they describe these substances as having the physical form of needles, arrows, pebbles, and slivers, which only the healers can see. Third, they have the ability to speak to specific */ /gangwasi* and argue with them. Lastly, they have a host of secondary skills involving knowledge of dietary prescriptions and prohibitions. As they put it, "we can tell the people how to eat properly."

Though not a central part of their ritual, the !Kung men routinely walk in fire and handle live coals without burning themselves. It is mainly the less experienced healers who do this. They walk in fire because, as one told Dick Katz, "Because *n/um* is hot like fire it makes you want to jump in. Because you don't know what is fire and what isn't. But only the young ones without brains do this" (Katz 1982:122).

How effective are these healing practices? Are the !Kung *n/um k''ausi* actually able to heal the sick by pulling out substances and by driving away the spirits of the dead? In thinking about this tricky question it is important to keep in mind that the !Kung healers operate with the same odds that medical doctors do: over 90 percent of all illnesses are self-limiting and would go away even if left untreated. With these kinds of odds to start off, the !Kung healers, like our own, have a high success rate.

The healing dances at which these performances take place are the main ritual activity of the Dobe !Kung. They occur from once a month to several times a week, depending on the season, the size of the camp, and other factors. The presence of sickness is not the only reason for dancing. These dances serve a social as well as a sacred function. In fact, they are in many ways like a party—a time for relaxing, socializing, and letting off steam. The sacred and healing purposes of the dance do not seem to be spoiled by the socializing; in fact, they may be aided by it. The !Kung say the stronger the singing, the better the *n/um*.

The sacred dance fire is lit after sundown, and the women singers arrange themselves in a circle around it. Around the women, the men dance, beating a circular path in the sand several inches deep. There is a strict division of labor in the dance. The women sing and tend the fire, and the men dance and enter trances. Occasionally a woman will dance with the men for a few turns, and very occasionally a woman healer will enter trance. However, the men insist that it is the women who are crucial to the success of the dance. Without their strong sustained singing, the *n/um* cannot boil and the men cannot heal.

The *n/um* songs, sung without words, have beautiful complex melodies. They include several versions of Giraffe and older songs, such as Gemsbok, Eland (my favorite), Mongongo, Rain, and several others. When I first saw Giraffe danced with its intricate melodies and rhythms, I assumed that it was a very old dance, going back beyond the memories of people. I was surprised to learn that, far from being old, the Giraffe dance was invented by a man named /Ti!kay, who was still alive at Chum!kwe. He gave Giraffe and two other dances to the people after //Gangwa had come to him in a dream. The basic dance form, however, must be very old. Prehistoric San rock paintings show people performing the same steps (Lewis-Williams 1981).

The first few hours of the dance are relaxed and sociable. Then, nearing midnight, one or more men begin to show the signs of trance: glassy stares, intense footwork, and heavy breathing. They start to sweat profusely. The other men call to the women *gu tsiu-, gu tsiu*—"pick it up, pick it up," and the women sing louder and more intensely. First one healer and then the others fall into trance and begin to cure. An ordinary dance might continue until two or three in the morning. On a good night the music and the singing will be so powerful that the dance is still going strong as the sun rises. On very special occasions a dance will go all night, right through the next day, and end the morning of the third day.

Becoming a Healer

Every young !Kung man aspires to become a healer, and a surprisingly large proportion of the men achieve this status. *N/um*, the !Kung say, is not the exclusive possession of a few. It was given by //Gangwa to all the !Kung. Almost half of the adult men have achieved the *!kia* (trance) state, and about a third of the women.

In seeking *n/um*, a young man must undergo a long and difficult training process. First he must find someone to train him—his father or uncle if they have *n/um*, or a nonrelated *n/um k"au*. The !Kung discourage the very young or immature from seeking *n/um*. They say that achieving the *!kia* state is extremely painful and should not be undertaken lightly. At dances the novices can be seen dancing intensely, staring straight forward and not engaging in the social chatter of the dance. The teacher will usually go into trance himself and then work on his pupil, rubbing sweat into key centers: the chest, belly, base of spine, and forehead.

But at a certain point one often sees the novices leave the dance and sit down at the edge trying to "come down" and regain their composure. They may reenter the dance, only to step out a few minutes later. I asked N!eishi, an experienced healer, why the novices always stop at this point. He replied, "*N/um* is not an easy thing. It is extremely difficult. As the *n/um* starts to build up inside you, the pain is intense. You are gasping for breath. You feel as if you are choking. The boys are afraid; they fear what will happen to them next."

"What are they afraid of?" I asked. "The pain? The unknown? The *gangwasi*?"

"Death," replied N!eishi.

The state is indeed painful, as I discovered on my one attempt to enter *!kia*. On further questioning the healers I was able to get a better sense of what they feared. It seems that there is both a psychological and a physical barrier, on the

A !Kung healer working himself into a !kia *state.*

one hand involving maximum physical exertion and on the other an acute fear of loss of control.

What *is* this barrier? I think the best way to understand it is to compare it to "the wall," the phenomenon marathon runners experience around mile 19 of a 26-mile run. You reach a point beyond which it seems physically impossible to go. If you do go on and finish the race, it is because you have tapped into physical and emotional resources you didn't know you had.

Achieving *!kia* for the first time seems to involve a similar kind of break-through. The young dancer must punch through his pain and anxiety by force of will to reach a new level of experience. This, I think, is what *!kia* and *n/um* are about. Even the most accomplished healers go through periods of doubt. As one man put it to Dick Katz,

> *N/um* is hot; mine is hot too. Others who say it is not have deceived you. Those without *n/um* may look at those who do *n/um* and say, "Why can't I do like that?" Now if I tell them that it's very painful, they say, "Oh, you're just fooling me. I still want to do *n/um!*" But then when they start, they see how painful it is, and then they stop because they fear it. This is how it was with me. I thought they were kidding me when they told me how painful *n/um* was. I tried *n/um*, and it was so painful that I stopped. And I even stopped going to dances for years because I feared *n/um*. Only after I got married did I try *n/um* again. This time [the pain] again came up in me, but I passed through it, and then *n/um* came to me. Now I have *n/um*. (Katz 1982:119)

Entering *k!ia*, however, is only the first step. Once in the trance, the novice's perceptions become acutely disoriented and his behavior becomes wild and erratic. He will run off into the bush gashing himself on branches or thorns, or worse, dance through the *n/um* fire itself, showering burning coals in every direction. The healers say that the young ones are still afraid of *n/um*; they can't control it, and they must be restrained. The teacher, now aided by other men and women, force the young man to lie down. They massage his body vigorously, always from the extremities to the torso, and on the torso towards the stomach, symbolically work-ing the boiling *n/um* back into its resting state in the pit of the stomach. (John Marshall's excellent film on the trance dance, "*N/um chai*" (1969) has a long sequence of a young trancer being aided in this way.)

With time, most of the men overcome their fear of *n/um*; they learn to control its effects and to make it work for them. (About a third of those who achieve *!kia*, however, do not continue on to become healers.) For those who succeed, the path is opened for them to explore new levels of reality and to perform a useful function for the community and for their families. Although they worry that the novice trancers will hurt themselves, parents are delighted when offspring become healers for, as one mother said,

> It is all right when they try to throw themselves into the fire. It shows the *n/um* is strong in them. This is good. If he has *n/um* he can take care of his children. If I am sick he can heal me.

THE WOMEN'S DRUM DANCE

In recent years a new dance has been gaining in popularity among the !Kung. Beginning at the turn of the century and centered at the !Goshe waterhole, the Women's Dance, *!Gwah tsi*, has been spreading rapidly. It was unknown to the Marshalls during their Nyae Nyae fieldwork in the 1950s. It reached Chum!kwe during the 1960s, and since then it has taken on the character of a social move-ment, gaining new converts every year. During the 1980s it even exceeded the Men's Giraffe Dance in popularity.

The Women's Drum Dance: !Gwahtsi.

In *!Gwah tsi* the roles of the Giraffe Dance are reversed. Women dance and enter trance, and men play a supporting role, beating complex rhythms on the long drum that is the central symbol of the dance. Dances may be held weekly, and when the new form reaches a settlement dances may occur nightly as new women join in. Typical dances involve 8 to 12 women, and several drummers working in relays. Two, three, or up to eight women may *!kia* at any one dance. Men enjoy the dance as drummers and spectators, and they may assist the women who enter trance.

Dances begin at nightfall, the sound of the drums summoning the people. The women arrange themselves in a semicircle, with the drummer off to one side. They sing the *!Gwah* songs and accompany the drumming with contrasting hand-clapping rhythms. Instead of dancing in a circle, the women dance in one place with short steps, swaying from side to side. The onset of the *!kia* state is heralded by a bout of intense trembling in the legs. The woman staggers and is held up by the other dancers. After a few minutes the woman collapses into a full *!kia*.

The women say that the *!Gwah* medicine lies in the stomach and the kidneys. When they dance, it rises in two routes, up the chest and the backbone, and when active it lodges in the cervical vertebrae. In *!kia* the woman is rubbed and massaged by the other women, but no healing of the kind commonly seen in the Giraffe Dance occurs in the Women's Dance. This is a major difference between the two forms.

Women entering *!kia* for the first few times seem to experience the same kind of pain and anxiety as the men do, but not to the same degree. They do not run off into the bush or try to fling themselves into the fire. They do behave erratically and thus require supervision. Frequently at this stage the helping women will cover the *!kia* woman's lap with a blanket and change her pubic apron. They say they do this because when a woman falls in *!kia* she is likely to expose herself.[6] The pubic apron of experienced women may be changed as well.

The *!Gwah tsi* is not primarily a healing dance as such, but rather a dance for introducing women to *!kia* and allowing them to go deeper into *!kia* in a supportive context. As one woman put it, "Most of us are just learning to *!kia*. We are new at entering it. It is like school for us. But the older ones do *kowhedile*."

This is true. After a period of training, many women go on to become healers. At special healings, women healers are now active, performing the laying on of hands and the pulling of sickness and seeing the *//gangwasi*, just as the men do. Often men and women healers work in teams on seriously ill people.

The source of this power, the women claim, is the *!gwah* plant, a short, stiff unidentified shrub. The roots are chopped up and boiled, and the tea drunk. It is only taken initially and not before every dance. So the active principle of the drug, if any, is not a prerequisite to *!kia*. I suspect that ingesting the infusion has a psychological rather than a psychochemical effect on the initiates.

The Drum Dance appears to have first entered the Dobe area from the east around 1915. The drum itself was borrowed from the Mbukushu, a Bantu-speaking farming people living in the Okavango swamps. The co-founder of the Drum Dance was a woman named /Twa, who was still alive in the 1960s. /Twa was generally acknowledged to be the most powerful healer, male or female, in the Dobe area. I interviewed her in 1964.

"The Drum Dance started with the Mbukushu, where my father was working," /Twa said. "The !Kung used to build them for the Mbukushu, so when it came here we knew how to make them. The one who was responsible for bringing it here was my husband, /Gau, who was traveling around. We started Drum together."

For years the Drum Dance was confined to !Kangwa and !Goshe, and the main practitioners were /Twa, her two daughters, and the people of !Goshe. Starting around 1960, it began to spread west, reaching /Xai/xai and Chum!kwe in the mid-1960s. When /Twan!a died in 1972 at an estimated age of 85, the dance had spread throughout the !Kung area and was rapidly supplanting the Giraffe Dance as the major !Kung ritual. At !Goshe today the women have even begun to admit men as trainees in a modified *!Gwah tsi* that contains elements of both male and female rituals.

Other forms of new rituals appear from time to time among the !Kung. A /Xai/xai man named /Gaugo left the area to work on a contract as a mine laborer in Johannesburg. He experienced a revelation there and rested and brought a highly entertaining new dance form back to /Xai/xai in 1967. Called Trees Dance, it involves a male leader barking orders in Fanagalong, the mine jargon, at a chorus line of women. The structure and premise of Trees Dance are strongly reminiscent of the famous Mine dances held in the mining compounds on Sundays. /Gau's male helpers at the dance are called "Bossboy" and "Foremana." The people of /Xai/xai danced Trees Dance for days on end in 1967–1968.

---

[6] *!Kia* experiences may also be symbolically connected with sexual arousal and orgasm.

/Twan!a putting n/um
into her pupil Chu!ko.

THREE MEDICINES: ONE BLOOD

Earlier I mentioned that the !Kung, though immersed in their own beliefs, are aware of and receptive to other theories of illness and health. Their Black neighbors, the Herero, Tswana, and Bayei, have well-developed beliefs in sorcery, and the !Kung have been struggling to accommodate these within their own explanatory system. They are less impressed with European theories of disease causation, but they have easily accepted the efficacy of European medicines, particularly antibiotics.

/Twan!a, the most charismatic of the !Kung healers, told me,

People were created by //Gangwan!n!a with different things to use, different skins, and different medicines. The Blacks have their medicine in divination and sorcery, the Europeans have their medicine in pills and steel needles, and the San have their medicine in the form of *kowhedile*. Different medicine, very different ways of living. But when you cut any one of them their blood flows the same color.

During the time of my fieldwork, there had been no Western missionary work among the Dobe !Kung, and thus there had as yet been no ideological attack from that quarter on !Kung beliefs. The beliefs of the Blacks have offered a far more fundamental challenge to the !Kung. Sorcery, the belief in the ability of one person to consciously do harm to another by magical means, explains misfortune in a very un-!Kung way. Central to !Kung belief is the concept of the //gangwasi as an external threat. The ghosts attack, and the living must unite to defend themselves. Thus the healing dance involves the whole body of the living in a struggle against an external enemy—the dead. Sorcery (and witchcraft) beliefs, by contrast, seek the source of misfortune *within* the community. A spouse, a kinperson, or a neighbor could be causing illness knowingly or unknowingly. Such beliefs set kin against kin and neighbor against neighbor. They divide the living into mutually suspicious camps and break down the solidarity of the community.

This new explanatory system now competes with the older theory of misfortune for dominance in !Kung thought. The struggle has put a great deal of strain on !Kung social relations. Among the more acculturated !Kung there is more interpersonal hostility, especially between the sexes. Beliefs in sorcery affects the !Kung in several major ways. Some injuries and illnesses of !Kung are interpreted to have been caused by Black sorcery. In other cases, !Kung have sought out Black diviners who, in return for payment, have diagnosed the source of illness as coming from living relatives of the !Kung. For further payment, the diviners will take appropriate countermeasures.

The flow of culture is not just one way. The Blacks are also impressed with !Kung healing techniques and believe in their efficacy. Blacks frequently ask !Kung healers to do a healing on their sick, and this type of work is usually accompanied by payment in cash or in kind.

That raises an interesting question: When !Kung healers diagnose Blacks' illnesses, which theory of disease causation do they employ? Do they see the source of illness in terms of the dead or the living?

There is some evidence that they use both theories. Blacks are not adverse to concepts of misfortune deriving from ancestors. In fact, a new syncretic form of explanation has emerged that combines sorcery and !Kung theories. A !Kung who is ill may accuse a !Kung neighbor of not propitiating his //gangwasi properly and of allowing them to bring sickness. Thus the source of illness remains the same—the dead—but a new element of human agency is introduced.

This kind of explanation is still not widespread, but it is becoming more common and may indicate a new, privatized theory of disease causation, congruent with new forms of private property and wage earning, where ownership is much clearer and the importance attached to sharing declines.

Another very important aspect of the changing conceptions of health and illness among the !Kung is the new professionalism of the healers. /Twan!a was one of the first paid healers. She has received goats, blankets, clothing, and money for her healing work with the Blacks. Other !Kung healers have followed suit, even traveling to commercial farming areas in Botswana to perform healings for San and Black workers.

But there very success has put new strains on the healers in their relationship to the community. In the past, n/um was freely given, and the rewards to the healers were manifold and diffuse. Personal satisfaction, the love and respect of family, and the gratitude of those they had "saved" are some of the positive themes mentioned by healers in interviews. But the interviews contain another theme, a recurrent complaint about other !Kung: they are *chi dole* (bad, strange) because they take the medicine for granted and don't pay for successful treatment. ≠Toma zho, a famous /Xai/xai healer (see Katz 1982:177–195), has started to make regular trips to the Ghanzi farms to cure and dance because at /Xai/xai "people haven't paid me anything."

When two cultures come into contact the problem arises of translating values from one to the other. This translation concerns tangibles—for example, how much tobacco for one antelope hide—but it can also concern intangibles like healing "services." In our discussion of *hxaro* (Chapter 7), we saw how the essence of *hxaro* was to resist the idea of exact equivalences, focusing instead on the value of the *social* relationship with the *hxaro* partner.

Putting a price tag on a healing removes it from the communal sphere. Payment for healing validates the healer in a different way, marking the value of his treatment by price, and the higher the price, the better the treatment. But once the healer has been paid, it is difficult for him or her to turn around and "do it for nothing." When a healing is done for pay it, in effect, belongs to the individual who paid for it, not to the community at large.

Not all healers share this view, however. Many continue to heal other !Kung as they always have, for free. They deplore the fact that some of their fellow healers are holding back.

The !Kung are rapidly entering the cash economy (see Chapter 10). The debate among healers illustrates graphically how individuals attempt to grapple at the level of consciousness with the wrenching changes that accompany the shift from a community-based economy to an economy based on the impersonal forces of the marketplace. It is this theme that we will address in the final chapters.

9/The !Kung and their neighbors

Since the 1920s, the !Kung have shared the Dobe area with Herero and Tswana pastoralists. These were tribal peoples, speaking Bantu languages, whose lives were not so very different from that of the !Kung. The Herero and Tswana grew crops, kept livestock, and made iron tools, but their social systems, like the !Kung's, were based on kinship, and neither people had developed markets, monarchs, or elaborate craft specialization.

The Tswana lived in chiefdoms with the beginnings of internal stratification, and the !Kung were immediately accorded a position at the bottom of the social scale, but in the Dobe area the San were not enserfed or enslaved; nor were they propelled into the cash economy.

Though subordinate, the San were not simply servants of the Blacks. In the early days, Tswana and !Kung men hunted side by side, each with bow and arrows, and in recent years Tswana and Herero women have been observed gathering wild plants alongside !Kung women in times of drought.

Since the time of the first Black visitors in the nineteenth century or earlier, the !Kung have been exposed to several important innovations: the use of metal tools and containers, the smoking of tobacco, and the raising of livestock and planting of crops. They adopted the first two with enthusiasm: iron tools and cooking utensils are universals among the !Kung, and everyone smokes tobacco when they can get it. In fact, the two innovations are combined in the !Kung's favorite smoking device, an empty rifle shell obtained from the Blacks with tobacco stuffed in one end and a grass stopper in the other. But the more basic economic changes of agriculture and livestock production did not take hold. By 1960 the !Kung still remained hunter-gatherers without herds or fields. They have, however, established social and economic ties with the Blacks, and these ties are the subject of this chapter.

The chapter introduces the Herero and Tswana, details their interactions with the !Kung, and explains how the lives of the !Kung have been affected by living as hunters in a world of nonhunters.

INTRODUCING THE HERERO AND THE TSWANA

The Hereros are the largest group of non-!Kung in the Dobe area. They are superb pastoralists, and their cattle herds number in the thousands. They also

119

Herero and !Kung women.

practice agriculture. They live in dispersed hamlets of two to six houses built around a cattle kraal. They practice a system of double descent with an individual belonging to both his or her father's and mother's lineages. Women enjoy relatively high status and frequently own and inherit cattle. The women wear a characteristic dress adapted from the early German missionaries: full-length, gaily colored dresses with many underskirts and petticoats and a matching three-cornered headdress or *tuku*.

Speaking a southwestern Bantu language, the Herero migrated south from Angola several centuries ago into what is now central Namibia. Growing strong from a combination of extensive cattle pastoralism and raiding, the Herero were a powerful and populous presence in southwest Africa when the German colonists arrived in the 1880s. But the Germans, through force and trickery, steadily encroached upon the Heroro lands. Finally, in desperation, the Herero arose in

1904 and killed some of the colonists. The Germans used this as a pretext for an all-out war of extermination. By the end of 1905, 60 percent of the estimated 80,000 Hereros had been killed by the Germans or had died of thirst in the Kalahari trying to escape the war. Several thousand survived the trek across the desert and sought refuge in the Tswana chiefdoms to the east, in the British sphere of influence. There the Herero survivors rebuilt their herds. It is the descendants of these refugees who form the bulk of the 250 Hereros who now live in the Dobe area. Work on the Herero cattle posts provides a major source of employment for the !Kung.

The BaTawana, one branch of the powerful BaTswana chiefdoms, are the overlords of the region. Although numerically small in the Dobe area, they are large cattle-holders and until recently dominated the administrative posts at both the chiefdom and the national government levels. In the Dobe area they live in dispersed hamlets similar to those of the Herero (who in fact adopted their house type from the Tswana). Elsewhere in Botswana, the other Tswanas traditionally live in large towns of up to 20,000 people.

Tswana language, social organization, and, especially, legal code provide models for the !Kung and other subject peoples to adopt. The court, or *kgotla*, of the Tswana headman has been an important element in dispute settlement since the 1940s.

The first Tswana reached the Dobe area in the 1970s on brief hunting expeditions. By 1900 the area had been allocated to two powerful Tswana families in a kind of feudal tenure, one receiving the area north of the /Ahas and the other the area to the south. Some decades passed before the first Tswana settled in the area.

In addition to these immigrants, there are small numbers of two other Bantu-speaking peoples in the Dobe area: the Mbukushu and the BeYei. Both live in the nearby Okavango swamps and are known collectively by the !Kung as *Goba*, a term generally applied to all non-Herero, non-Tswana Blacks.[1]

Actual settlements of the Dobe area by outsiders only began in the 1920s, and even by 1948, when a headmanship was established, the total number of non-!Kung residents probably was under 50. Since 1950 the numbers have steadily increased. Their presence has affected the !Kung in several ways. The Herero and Tswana immigrants have built homesteads, deepened and fenced off the waterholes, hired !Kung men as laborers, and in some cases have begun to court and marry !Kung women. We will look at each of these impacts in turn.

ECOLOGICAL CHANGE

As the Hereros and Tswana came with their cattle to settle most of the waterholes of the Dobe area, major ecological changes occurred. First, they deepened the wells to ensure a water supply for their stock, and fenced off the deep pits to

---

[1] American Blacks, interestingly, are classified as whites by the !Kung. Japanese are called Machapani or the "zhu/twa/onsi" (the San Europeans).

Ecological change: !Kung men watering Herero cattle from a deepened well.

prevent the cattle from falling in. The !Kung have benefited in some ways from this work: it gives them a cleaner and more abundant water supply. But the presence of cattle has had the effect of lowering the water table and of turning once-verdant *molapos* into dustbowls.

The effect on vegetation and insect lift has also been considerable. The cattle and goats have destroyed the grass and leafy shrub cover within a three-kilometer radius of the permanent waterholes, and a cover of thorny runners and bushes has replaced it. Also, each cattle post has a massive permanent population of house-flies that people learn to tolerate. Farther afield, grass cover and game still persist, and here one can see the northern Kalahari environment as it used to be.

Cattle and goats don't compete directly with humans for edible plant species. Animals cannot ingest, for example, the famous mongongo nut. Much of the !Kung's vegetable diet remains accessible to them despite the inroads of the cat-tle. At one waterhole, however, the cattle are a real menace. For reasons unknown, the cattle of /Xai/xai have developed a taste for human clothing and will eat your laundry right off the line if it left untended. Washing is jealousy guarded, and some of the !Kung have stockaded their camps to keep the marauders away. No one has suggested a plausible explanation for this puzzling phenomenon, which has been the subject of several cases in the tribal court. The local Tswana and Herero believe it is sorcery. The !Kung and I were inclined to agree.

WORK RELATIONS

In 1968 there were 4500 cattle and 1800 goats in the Dobe area, 95 percent in Tswana and Herero hands. These large herds could not be managed effectively by the Blacks themselves because they were so few in number, and so, many !Kung men were brought into service as cowherds. The !Kung, usually boys between the ages of 15 and 25, but some much older, would work with the cattle owner, take their meals with the Herero family, and sleep in the Heroro hamlet. Each worker was given a donkey to ride, a store-bought outfit of shirt, pants, and shoes, and a blanket to sleep on. If he was married he could bring his wife and family to live with him. The wages, if any, were minimal, but at the end of a year's service, if his work was satisfactory, the herder might receive a female calf of his own as payment. If the calf survived to maturity and proved fertile, the offspring were also his, and with luck they could form the basis of a small herd. Because of high bovine mortality, however, this rarely occurred. The real advantage of employment for the !Kung herdsman was not the long-term benefits, which were risky at best, but rather the short-term gain of being able to offer hospitality to his relatives at the cattle post.

The Herero and Tswana lived in kin-based societies like the !Kung, and they placed a high value on offering hospitality to visitors and neighbors. Every !Kung in the Dobe area had a son, nephew, or other relative working for the Blacks, and all the San paid regular visits to one cattle post or another to drink the milk.

The milk is never taken fresh. It is always poured into large gourds or calabashes containing a yogurt-like bacterial culture. It may be taken as whole sour milk, or the cream may be taken off to be churned into butter and the skim sour milk drunk. I found the whole sour milk (in Herero, *kamaihi*, in !Kung, *ku n!um*—literally, ripe milk) a tasty and refreshing drink. An Herero neighbor delivered a bottle of it to our camp every day. The skim milk, by contrast, was sour in the extreme, and only the hardy could enjoy it.

Another benefit of the Herero presence was the distribution of meat. Cattle from the large Herero herds sometimes fell prey to lions, leopards, or wild dogs. Whatever meat could be salvaged from the kill was distributed to the !Kung. More frequently, especially in the spring, the cattle would eat an attractive but highly poisonous plant called *mogau* and would die from the effects. The meat was unaffected by the poison, and the !Kung received the bulk of it. There were periods at /Xai/xai when the consumption of beef from this source considerably exceeded the meat produced by the !Kung's own hunting efforts.

Although many !Kung men worked for Hereros on the cattle and lived with them for years, few succeeded in becoming pastoralists in their own right. For most, working for the Blacks and being part of a client group was a phase in their lives. After a while they collected their families and possessions and returned to rejoin a parent's camp, a move which, however, might take them only a few hundred meters away.

For some, the work relation evolves into a kind of clientship, which could be a lifelong relationship. The client and his master live side by side, their children grow up together speaking each other's languages, and for the !Kung client a process of deculturation may begin. The !Kung may begin to identify more closely with Herero than with !Kung. In some cases this kind of co-residence and friendship leads to the marriage of !Kung and Blacks.

!Kung churning butter at an Herero village.

INTERMARRIAGE

In 1968 a small but significant number of !Kung women, about eight in all, were married to Herero and Tswana men. In addition, there were many more cases of Herero and Tswana young men having affairs with married and unmarried !Kung women. There were no !Kung men married to Black women, although we did hear of a few affairs involving !Kung men and Herero women.

!Kung women marrying Black men faced a number of problems. First, there was the question of status difference: marrying a Black man was definitely a step up. As one !Kung woman put it, "I married our masters." Second, there was the question of translating between the norms of the two kinship systems. How the Herero relatives would accept the !Kung woman was one concern, but equal in importance was the question of how the !Kung relatives would accept their Herero in-law. Finally, there was the question of the children: Would they be raised as Herero or !Kung? Who would decide?

From the Herero point of view, marrying a !Kung woman had advantages and disadvantages. Dobe was a frontier area with few amenities. The Herero settlers were far from the main Herero community. It was hard to convince a prospective Herero bride to come out to the Dobe area, far from relatives and friends. The !Kung, by contrast, were right there and used to the rigors of bush life. In fact, they found life on a Herero cattle post downright luxurious. Second, marrying a Herero involved elaborate negotiations and the payment of a large bride price; no similar payment was required for a !Kung bride. Third, the !Kung girls in their later teens were attractive and vivacious and were reputed by !Kung and Herero boys alike to be good lovers.

But there were disadvantages as well. The !Kung girls, though undeniably attractive, were by Herero standards free spirits. Herero gender relations were patriarchal, or at least *more* patriarchal than the egalitarian !Kung. Despite their lower status in the eyes of the Herero, the !Kung girls were not about to conform to the subservience and deference expected of them by their Herero in-laws. This was often a source of friction between Black husbands and their !Kung wives.

The question of bride price was also a double-edged sword. The dilemma it created is discussed by Gutayone, a Tswana man who married a !Kung woman and then found unexpected complications.

When I married /Twa, at first we were very happy together. We loved each other and she worked hard around the house. But later when we had a fight she would go away and live with her people for weeks at a time. We always made up, and continued to live together well, but then I had a terrible thought: if we had children and had a fight, what would stop her from taking the children and leaving me flat? Nothing!

Soon after that the matter came to a head when /Twa became pregnant. But what to do? I discussed it with my family, and my mother suggested we pay her people bride wealth (*bogadi*) for her. This would ensure that any children born would belong to our lineage. But another problem came up, who to give the *bogadi* to? /Twa was an orphan. Her parents and older brothers were dead. In our custom you give it to the lineage (*loshika*) on behalf of the girl's family, but the !Kung have no such unit. Each family is independent. /Twa's closest relative was a man named Kumsa, her mother's brother. My father and I went to him and said, "*Mi ≠tum*," using the !Kung term for father-in-law, "today I want to pay you *bogadi* for your child /Twa and for the child in her womb and for any future children."

Kumsa replied, "I don't know what you are talking about. What is this thing? What would I do with cattle? I live in the bush."

I said, "Cows are useful. You can keep them with the herd of the Blacks, who will take care of it for you."

After much talk, Kumsa finally agreed, and we transferred a heifer from our herd to that of a Herero near where Kumsa was living. Later Kumsa sold it and used the money to buy a donkey and a saddle and clothes. But we were satisfied. His acceptance of the cow meant that we had a right to /Twa's children if a dispute ever came up."

Whether Gutayone's fears were justified, I can't say, but his two sons, now in their twenties, have both been raised as Tswanas and think of themselves as Tswanas. Both, however, married !Kung girls when they grew up. In general, children of these mixed marriages grow up speaking both parental languages, but their identity was firmly with the dominant group. The boys tended to marry !Kung girls and the girls tended to marry Herero, but the numbers were too small to make any definite statements.

SWARA AND THE *SARWA*

One area of potential tension in Black-!Kung marriages, or for that matter, in all interethnic marriages, is the relationship between the husband on the one hand and the brothers and male relatives of the wife on the other. The husband from the dominant group in effect takes a woman away from the subordinate group, a potential bride for some local man. Resentment, open conflict, or worse could ensue unless some special steps were taken to smooth over this tricky relationship.

The Herero and Tswana use a special kinship term, *swara*, to apply to brothers-in-law created by intermarriage. This term and the behavior associated with it have proven so popular that the term is used informally as well for brothers-in-law among Blacks and !Kung themselves. *Swara* is a term associated with behaviors of extreme, almost exaggerated cordiality. Greetings are accompanied by jovial hand-shaking and backslapping, and sometimes include bawdy joking. The term is also used by a Herero with any !Kung man whose sister he is sleeping with, the implication being, "This is not just a casual affair, we are almost brothers-in-law." This joking and cordiality is quite out of character for !Kung brothers-in-law. As we saw in Chapters 5 and 6, the *tun!ga–tun!gama* relationship, referring to wife's brother or sister's husband (man speaking), is an avoidance relationship, not a joking one. !Kung men related this way are supposed to show respect, not joviality.

What then is the function of the term *swara*? The widespread use of the term evidently fulfills a need in interethnic relations for defusing the anger between wife's brothers of the subordinate group and their sisters' husbands from the dominant group. There is, however, an important hidden agenda in the use of this term. The term *swara* is used reciprocally: both Blacks and !Kung call each

*Herero giving cow's meat
from a lion kill to the
!Kung.*

other *swara*, implying that *either man could give his sister in marriage to the
other*. When !Kung and Blacks call each other *swara* they are sharing a joke: "You
gave me your sister today, I may give you my sister tomorrow."

This of course is not true. Despite the apparent reciprocity, the dominant group
will not give sisters in return to a subordinate group. It would be unthinkable for a
Herero or Tswana girl to marry a !Kung boy, and none have so far. Therefore the
term *swara* is a mystification hiding a basic inequality behind a show of equality
and reciprocity.

But the most fascinating aspect of the *swara* relationship has yet to be mentioned: Where did the term come from? It is not a !Kung word; nor is it Herero
or Tswana. In fact, it does not appear as the basic term for brother-in-law in any
African language.[2] The term *swara* is of Afrikaans origin, the language of the
Boer settlers of South Africa. It is a direct descendant of the Afrikaans word for
brother-in-law, *swaer*, related to the Dutch term *zwager*. This derivation opens a
very interesting area of explanation of how the term came into being in the first
place. The modern Afrikaners oppose intermarriage, and a White can go to jail
in South Africa for even sleeping with a non-White, but their ancestors did not
share this abhorrence of "miscegenation." On the contrary, history tells us that
the Afrikaner men actively sought liaisons with San, Khoi, and Bantu women on

_____

[2] In some it appears as a secondary term, but its derivation is the same as for the !Kung
(see text).

the frontier. Since both the term *swara* and the associated behavior are not indigenous to either the San or the Herero-Tswana, it is reasonable to assume that
the term and the bahavior had their beginnings with the Boer frontier settlers of
earlier times. Marrying a woman of the local people turns a potential enemy into
a brother-in-law. And your children tie you together even more strongly, but the
tenseness of the situation must be papered over with cordiality. One can imagine
the term *swara* traveling down through generations and spreading throughout
southern Africa, as men of one society moved into territory held by another. The
tension of hostility versus friendship remains in the *swara* tie, as does the remarkable ambiguity between equality/reciprocity on the one hand and inequality/
hierarchy on the other.

10/Perceptions and directions of social change

Despite their history of contact with Whites and Blacks, the !Kung were still relatively isolated when I first encountered them in 1963. They had very hazy notions of the world beyond their periphery. For example, no one I spoke to in 1963 had ever heard of Africa. They were surprised to learn that they lived on a large body of land called Africa. They *had* heard of South Africa, however. They called it *Johanni*, after Johannesburg, the place where the mine laborers went. More striking was the fact that none of the !Kung were aware of the Atlantic Ocean, which was less than 800 kilometers (500 miles) due west of Dobe. I asked them if they knew of a body of water that was so large that if you stood on one side you couldn't see the other. After much discussion they pointed north to the Okavango River, rather than west to the Atlantic.

But a third experience brought home to me how unfamiliar the !Kung were with the ways of the wider world. In 1964 I hired Koshitambo, one of the most sophisticated and well-traveled !Kung. He had made frequent trips to Maun, the tribal capital, as a valet to the local headman, Isak; he loved to make jokes in Setswana and Herero, and seemed to be as knowledgeable about the world as any !Kung. I agreed to pay him £10 for two months' work, a reasonable sum in those days, and on pay day I handed him an envelope containing two crisp £5 notes. Koshitambo looked puzzled and appeared upset, but I thought nothing of it and went on with my business. Ten minutes passed, and I caught a glimpse of him sitting forlornly at the edge of the camp, the £5 notes in his hand.

"What's the matter?" I asked Koshitambo.

"Oh, nothing," he said, hesitating.

"Yes there is, I can see something is wrong."

"Oh, /Tontah," Koshitambo finally blurted out, "/Tontah, you disappoint me. You said you were going to pay me ten monies, but instead you have paid me only two!"

It took fifteen minutes and all my limited linguistic powers to explain to Koshitambo that those two scraps of legal tender indeed constituted "ten monies" and not just two. The idea of money, of paper money, of different denominations of paper money, and of convertibility all had to be carefully put across before a pale smile broke on Koshitambo's face and he pocketed the money.

Despite the changes, the !Kung entered the decade of the 1960s with their kinship, productive, and land-tenure systems relatively intact. They gave birth, raised

A !Kung, a Canadian, and an Herero: an old-style anthropological mug shot.

their children, married, grew old, prayed to their gods and buried their dead in ways that were similar to what they had done for hundreds of years. This is certainly not to say that the !Kung had been static or unchanging. Their way of life had its own rhythms of change, and the arrival of the Whites and the longer contacts with the Blacks had introduced many new elements. But the pace of these changes was sufficiently slow that with time they could be absorbed into the existing structures and world view. Their systems did not break under the force of these changes; they bent and adapted.[1]

But in the 1970s the tempo of change accelerated, and new changes kept arriving before the previous ones could be absorbed. The capacity of the !Kung to absorb these developments without shattering was being tested to the limit. It is these fundamental changes that will be explored in this chapter.

We will first try to look at the outside world through !Kung eyes. How do they perceive the coming of the Blacks and Whites? Then we will explore how

---

[1] For the reasons given, I fundamentally disagree with the thesis of Schrire (1980) and Wilmsen (1978, 1981) that prehistoric contact with herders, some as early as A.D. 1000, fundamentally altered the character of !Kung society long before 1900. If true, there should be an abundance of prehistoric evidence of cattle and goat bones in the Dobe area. Such evidence, despite concerted efforts to find it, is almost totally lacking.

they are attempting to adapt to agriculture, wage labor, schools, and changes in land tenure.

PERCEPTIONS OF THE WHITE MAN

Well into the 1970s the !Kung still retained a vigorous sense of themselves as a people and their special status in relation to outsiders. They called themselves *zhu/twasi*, "real" or "genuine" people, a term they grudgingly extended to San of other language groups elsewhere in the Kalahari—the Nharo, /Gwi, and !Ko— but not to their Black and White neighbors.

It took over a year of fieldwork before I could speak !Kung well enough to find out how the !Kung thought of me and the people I represented—the Whites —and where we fitted into their scheme of things. The picture was not flattering: very matter of factly, they considered us to be wild animals. One day in late 1964 I was interviewing //Kokan!a, the wise and playful wife of ≠Toma//gwe, about animal classification.

"Wild animals we call *!hohm*," she said. "Lions, leopards, cats, hyenas, and wild dogs we call *!hohm atsi*—wild things of the bush. Tswanas, Gobas, Hereros, and Europeans like you, /Tontah, we call *!hohmsa chu/o*, wild things of the village."

This came as a great revelation to me. "What exactly are the *!hohm*?"

"We call all creatures who are different from us *!hohm* because when they speak we cannot understand a word. *!hohm a tsi* are the animals that kill people. We don't understand their language either, so we call them *!hohm*."

"I don't quite understand. Do you mean you don't hear their language?" I asked.

Rakudu, a congenial and very intelligent !Kung man from Mahopa, interjected, "It's not quite so simple. The Blacks and Whites we don't understand at all. But the wild animals of the bush, we can understand them a little. When the *!hohm a tsi* call each other we understand what they say. They are saying, 'Come, come join me in enjoying this food.'

"We called the Blacks and the Whites *!hohm* long ago because we were afraid of them like we were afraid of wild animals. Today we don't fear them. We call them by their names. *Dama* (Herero), *≠Tebe* (Tswana), */Ton* (European)."

//Koka was right. Listening in on !Kung conversations, I heard the terms *!hohm* and its singular, *!homa*, used in everyday speech for Whites and Blacks, without derogatory intent. The older fear had been replaced by a familiarity, yet a definite distance remained.

The !Kung were fascinated by Western technology, which they called */tondiesi*, White Man's expertise or skill. They loved to ride on trucks most of all, and developed a lively curiosity about how things worked. I once asked the !Kung to name as many parts of the truck as they could. This proved to be an interesting exercise because the !Kung had to assemble vocabulary from several areas— anatomy, dress, and hunting technology—in order to describe the various parts. The headlights were called */gasi*—eyes, and the hood was called the *tsi*—mouth;

Fascination with Western technology: !Kung peering under the hood of a Land Rover.

the tires were the */gwesi*—shoes or sandals. Gasoline was called *n/i*, literally vegetable oil or butter; it was also called *!kaitoro*, a derivation from the word *petrol*. Most other parts of the truck were not named at all, or the English-derived names were used. The truck itself was called *do*, the !Kung word for metal. Tin cans were also called *do*.

Tape recorders were another source of wonderment for the !Kung. They were always asking to listen to tapes recorded at other villages and to *n/wi e dumsi*—literally, "collect our throats"—so that they could listen to themselves on the tape. One woman even went into trance while listening to a tape of the Women's Drum Dance (see also Katz 1982:187–191).

Some forms of Western high-tech were the subject of intense discussion. For example, Dobe lay on the flight path for jet planes from South Africa to Angola. Flying so high that they were almost invisible from the ground, the aircraft left vapor trails at 35,000 to 40,000 feet. One day Tsau, a leading /Xai/xai man, and I watched as a plane came over.

"What *is* that thing up there with the long tail?" asked Tsau.

"It's a 'fly machine,'" I answered, using the term !Kung used for airplane. "But it is flying so high that you can't see it."

"That's what I thought it was," explained Tsau, in all seriousness. "Some *zhu/wasi* deceived me. You know what they said? That the Whites were sending messages to each other on long rolls of paper. In the south they could take a great roll of

/Twan!a and other !Goshe people listening to a tape of one of their healing dances.

paper covered with writing and fire it out of a giant gun. It would stream over to the north and land. Then they would cover it with new writing and fire it back to the south." Never, I thought, had toilet paper been put to such an imaginative use.

Artificial satellites, which had begun to appear in the Kalahari skies after 1957, were also a topic of discussion. Remember that my fieldwork began only five years after the first satellite had appeared. One starry night I was camped in the bush with two men named /Gau, one young and one old, when a Sputnik slowly crossed the sky. As we watched its progress excitedly, I asked each of them what they thought it was.

Young /Gau spoke with feeling. "The elders have told me that when you see a star moving like that it means that war is coming from the west and going to the east."

Not a bad answer I thought, thinking about the Cold War and the arms race. "And what do you think it means?" I asked the older /Gau.

"I don't know what the elders say. They never said anything to me. All I know is when I see something like that I think the Whites sure have powerful *n/um* to make the stars move!"

In less than a decade, the isolation of the !Kung disappeared and their percep tions about and knowledge of the outside world changed rapidly. Young men began to travel out of the area to work on mines and farms, and they brought back wondrous tales of far-off places.

The same /Gau who had spoken so gravely of the satellites was a 25-year-old man who had never been farther than 100 miles from home. In July 1964 I hired him to be my assistant on an archeological dig near Lusaka Zambia, 500 miles east of Dobe. /Gau was eager for the chance to go to some of the world that he had heard about but never seen. He underwent a profound change on the trip. Arriving in Maun, the tribal capital, clad only in a *chuana*, the leather breechclout, /Gau expressed intense embarrassment. I bought /Gau an outfit—khaki shirt, shorts, socks, and shoes. He balled his *chuana* in his fist and heaved it with all his might into the Okavango River, saying, "I'm never going to wear that thing again as long as I live."

"I wouldn't bet on it, /*Gau*," I said.

The trip to Zambia lasted five weeks. /Gau was exposed to one staggering novelty after another: tarred roads, street lights, running water, and railroad trains were only a few. After three weeks /Gau took to his bed. Whether it was sickness or culture shock I could not tell. But when /Gau returned to Dobe he recovered almost immediately. And soon he was eager to share his experiences with his kin. At the same time, he was awed by the problem of how to put all of this new world into words, how to convey to his listeners a sense of what he saw. Since 1964 many !Kung have made such trips, and the experiences /Gau describes are commonplace, but then it was all, as he put it, "strange and fearful."

We drove and drove and drove and drove, through the country of the Gobas, the Damas, the Tswanas, and then we came to people who were San like ourselves, with our faces and our skin. They even had quivers on their shoulders like us, and yet when they spoke I could not understand a word of them. I had no *!kun!as* in common with them, no kinsmen among them. When we spoke we had to speak in Setswana. Then we left that place and came to a fence that stretched far in each direction. Men with guns and clothing the color of sand opened the gate and let us through. Then a strange thing happened. The road transformed itself. A giant black snake with a smooth back came up, and we rode on his back. He twisted and turned but we always stayed on his back; we never left him. Riding on that snake's back we went as fast as the wind.

We got to a big village of those people and stopped. We were dying of hunger by that time, and /Tontah made us go into a house and sit down on a chair with a table in front of it. A man who was not a relative of /Tontah came and brought food in a dish. There were three different kinds of food on one bowl. We had to eat it in a strange way. A metal thing shaped like a lizard's forefoot was given to me. I had to spear food with it and bring it to my mouth. It was very hard, but I learned to do it. The other things at this table—knives, cups, spoons—we have in our country too.

Metal is everywhere. When you twist metal, water comes out. You sleep on metal. When night comes giant metal flashlights as tall as trees come on and make the black snake's back shine like day. The people of this country refuse night. They reject it and push it back with light. Even in their houses there are flashlights everywhere.

But one creature of metal frightened me the most. It made the ground shake like a giant herd of wildebeest fleeing for their lives. It had one eye living in its face, like a ghost. It was bigger than many elephants, but walked on wheels like a truck. It had its path of metal and no one could make it go left or right. A fire was in its belly and black smoke breathed from its head. When it stopped it vomited people, and then ate more people. /Tontah was not afraid of it and said let's go in it. I refused. Then I said all right but feared it would kill me. I got in and sat still. When it started to move I wanted to get off. /Tontah made me stay on and so, fearing for my life, I lived.

After that I became ill and lay in my bed for many days. /Tontah took care of me and gave European n/um. Then /Tontah brought me back to Dobe; the medicine men and women worked me and worked me and revived me. Today I am just like myself again but happy to be alive and happy to be home.

Experiences like /Gau's gave the younger generations of !Kung a changed outlook from that of their parents. They came to handle cash with confidence and would speak of the relative merits of Johannesburg, Francistown, and Windhoek as places to find work. New technology such as transistor radios expanded their horizons even further.

I think it is fair to say that in the 1960s there were genuine disagreements among the !Kung on the desirability of change. Many !Kung expressed a fondness for their way of life and a love of the t'si—the bush. They said that in the bush you can always find food and game; in the bush you are free to live as you please. An equal number of !Kung, like young /Gau mentioned above, expressed a fear and dislike of the bush. The bush is hunger, said one man; it is heat and thirst, said another.

As time went on, more and more !Kung shifted to the latter view. They wanted money and the things that it could buy. They wanted donkeys to ride on and goats and cattle. But wanting is one thing, and getting is quite another.

TRANSITION TO FARMING AND HERDING

At the time of my first field trip in 1963, the Dobe area !Kung appeared to be full-time hunter-gatherers, with no agriculture or livestock (except as !Goshe). As the fieldwork proceeded, however, a more realistic picture emerged of the "pristine" nature of the Dobe area. I learned that most of the men had had experience herding cattle at some point in their lives, and that many men had owned cattle and goats in the past. Further, the !Kung were no strangers to agriculture. Many had learned the techniques by assisting Black neighbors, and in years of good rainfall had planted crops themselves. However, because of the extreme unreliability of the rainfall, none of them had succeeded in establishing themselves on an agricultural basis. The same pattern occurred with livestock raising. Men often obtained cattle or goats in payment for working for the Blacks, but only a few families had set themselves up as herders independent of a Black patron.

In all, the !Kung planted 10 different crops, including gourds, marijuana, sugarcane, and beans, but by far the most important crops—those planted by 50 or more families—were maize, melons, sorghum, and tobacco. Surprisingly, tobacco was the most frequently planted. It is also the most difficult of the four to grow, requiring deep shade and daily watering. The fact that the !Kung devoted so much of their farming effort to a nonfood crop suggests that the motive of increasing their food supply was not uppermost in their minds.

Sorghum was the most successful food crop, and those who planted it enjoyed a 50 percent rate of success, compared to 35 percent for maize. The government's Agricultural Extension Department even distributed bags of drought-resistant sorghum seed to !Kung and other marginal farmers during the 1967 and 1968 growing seasons.

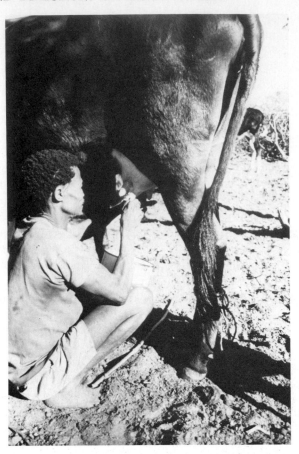

/Xashe milking a cow from his new herd, 1980.

Despite these efforts, agriculture continues to be a very risky proposition for the Dobe area !Kung. Only at !Goshe, where the !Kung enjoy the patronage of an influential Tswana-Yei cattleman, has agriculture begun to provide a significant proportion of the subsistence.

Unlike farming, livestock production is an economically viable adaptation in the Kalahari, and it continues to be the economic mainstay of Botswana. Some form of small-scale herding represents the main hope for the future development of San communities. During 1967–1969 only about 100 head of cattle and 155 goats were owned by !Kung in the Dobe area, representing about 2 percent of the cows and 8 percent of the goats in the district (see Chapter 9). Only six !Kung families owned the minimum number of livestosk to form a viable herd, and of these, only one man had set up with his family as independent farmer-herders. Most of the other people let their animals run with the herds of their Black neighbors.

A goat herd is easier to manage, and several families have built kraals and assembled small herds consisting of their own goats and those of their relatives.

These families put the children of the camp to work herding and watering the goats while the adult members combine farming with gathering and hunting. These are the modest beginnings of animal husbandry among the !Kung on their own, not as employees or clients of Black masters.

The possession of a herd of goats or cattle, or of a field of maize and melons, puts !Kung farmer-herders in a difficult position. First, their mobility is restricted by the need for daily supervision of the animals. It is not as easy for family members to go on an extended foraging trip or to pay visits to relatives at distant camps. Someone must always remain with the animals. Second, there are daily tasks to be performed, and the children are pressed into service. Draper (1976) has described how the children in the sedentary !Kung villages are put to work tending the animals or helping with chores, a contrast with their carefree life in the bush camps. A more subtle change noted by Draper (1975) concerns the separation of men and women in daily work and the confining of the latter much closer to home. In bush camps both women and men go far afield in the food quest. In village life, the men maintain their mobility, following the herds, but the women become housebound, with more of their time spent alone with their children and less with peers on common productive tasks. Perhaps the beginnings of the subordination of women can be glimpsed here in the reorganization of household work loads around the demands of farming and herding (see Lee 1975).

The Case of Debe and Bo

There is a great deal of tension between those families of !Kung who have begun to farm and herd and their relatives who continue the foraging life. There are real contradictions between the organization and ideology of farming and the organization and ideology of foraging. The most important of these is the contradiction between *sharing*, or generalized reciprocity, which is central to the hunting and gathering way of life, and the *saving*, or husbandry of resources, which is equally central to the farming and herding way of life. As we saw in Chapter 4, the food brought into a !Kung camp is shared out immediately with residents and visitors alike; for herders to do the same with their livestock, or farmers with their harvested grain, would quickly put them out of business.

How people grappled with these contradictions on the ground was very interesting. Sometimes they made surprising choices. For example, there were two enterprising !Kung men at Mahopa, one named Debe, the other Bo. Debe assembled a small herd of goats and cattle and appeared to be on his way to becoming a successful herder. But when meat was scarce his relatives would visit from /Xai/xai, and under heavy social pressure, Debe would slaughter one goat after another until after several years he sold or gave away his remaining herd, saying that the responsibilities were too heavy. Debe was also successful as a farmer, but his relatives always seemed to appear on his doorstep right at harvest time to consume his harvested crops. Later he tried to enlist the help of his relatives in building a larger field so that they could plant crops together for all of them to eat. But they were so reluctant that Debe in disgust *hired* a Black for wages to help him clear the land and build the brush fence—the first case we know of in which a San paid wages to a Tswana. Oscillating between exhorting his kinfolk to help him farm and hiring an outsider, Debe seemed to be caught in the contradictions between a communalistic and an individualistic style of work relations.

The second man was Bo, the leader of the only group whose members have established themselves as independent farmer-herders. Bo took great pride in his herd of six cows and his fields of maize and melons, and he emphasized to all who would listen that he was on his own and not under Black patronage. Bo was also a rational man, and when his many kinsmen and affines came to his hamlet to share in his good fortune, he fed them a fine meal, offered his fire for overnight, and sent them on their way the next morning with a handful of his home-grown tobacco. Bo knew that nothing could put him out of business more quickly than the arrival of kin on extended visits, so he sent them on their way. The effects of this were striking: people spoke of Bo as stingy and far-hearted; he became feared, and there were mutterings that he had learned techniques of sorcery from Black diviners. So Bo became a successful but very isolated farmer-herder. Finally, in 1970, Bo had had enough. He sold all his cattle and other stock for cash, packed his things, and walked across the border to settle at Chum!kwe in Namibia. It was factors such as these, and not simply ecological limitations, that were preventing more !Kung from moving into farming and herding during the 1960s and 1970s. But even more dramatic changes were on the horizon.

WAGE WORK AND MIGRANT LABOR

During the period 1900–1979 migrant labor in the gold fields of South Africa was a main source of income for hundreds of thousands of African men drawn from Lesotho, Swaziland, Mozambique, Botswana, and as far away as Angola and Malawi. In some areas half the adult men are away in the mines at any given moment.

This practice reached the Dobe area in the late 1950s. By 1968, 15 Dobe area men, about 10 percent of the adult male population, had made the trip to Johannesburg; 8 of them had made two or more trips, and 1 man had signed on for 5 of the 9-month tours of duty. Men reported wages of between R12 and R18 per month (18 to 25 American dollars), but from this total were deducted the worker's off-hours canteen and bar bills, so that when the Dobe area workers were paid off at the end of their contracts, most brought home only between R25 and R40 in total.

In order to go to Johanni, Dobe area men had to walk out 100 kilometers to the main road at Nokaneg and hitch a ride north to the Witwatersrand Native Labour (Wenela) recruiting depot at Shakawe. After receiving a cursory medical examination, they would wait along with 150 other men for the weekly flight to the mines. At Johannesburg they were sent to one of the 40 or so giant Rand gold mines. The shorter men were classified for surface work at lower pay; the taller and huskier ones were chosen for the more dangerous and better-paid underground work. Returning home after 9 months' work, the men were paid off in Shakawe, where a variety of home-brew joints and prostitutes were waiting to relieve them

One hundred and fifty miles north of Dobe is the recruiting depot for migrant laborers to the South African mines.

of part of their pay. Many returning workers have brought gonorrhea back to the Dobe area as a result. With the rest of their money the men purchased clothes, shoes, saddles, blankets and yard goods, and sometimes donkeys to make their way back to the home area.

The system of remitting mine wages back to families in the rural areas was unknown among the Dobe San. There was no post office, and neither the workers nor their wives could read or write. Instead, the !Kung had developed a standard method for translating the values gained through wage work back into significant values in the *hxaro* exchange system.

When young Bo returned to !Kangwa in September 1968, he was dressed to kill in fedora, plaid shirt, undershirt, sport jacket, long pants with cowboy belt, underpants, new shoes, and socks. Over the next few days his wardrobe dwindled as each item of clothing appeared in turn in the costume of a friend or relative. By the third day Bo himself was strolling around dressed only in his undershirt and his leather *chuana*. Bo had given away his entire wardrobe in the *hxaro* network, and we enjoyed seeing one of his kinsmen appear in fedora and *chuana*, another in sport jacket and *chuana*, and so on.

In 1967 the first store opened in the Dobe area, at !Kangwa, operated by Greek traders. Housed in the first modern building ever constructed in the !Kangwa Valley, the store sold mealie meal, soap, kerosene, clothing, saddles, and dry goods at inflated prices and purchased cattle from the Herero at reduced prices. The San had few, if any, cattle to sell, but five young men were hired for wages to tend and water the purchased cattle. The pay was only R6 to R8 per month ($8.40 to $11.20), but even this small amount has had a major impact in a world without cash.

The major impact of the store on both the San and their Black neighbors came from a single store-bought commodity—sugar. Sugar is the prime ingredient in the potent home-brewed beer (actually a form of mead) that is the centerpiece of a new culture that has sprung up around the !Kangwa store. The beer, called *khadi*, is a clear amber beverage that looks and tastes like a sparkling hard cider. It is made from brown sugar and *Grewia* berries, with fermentation induced by a mixture of bee earth, honeycomb, and honey called *seretse*. A number of !Kung women have set themselves up as beer entrepreneurs, buying the sugar at the store and selling the product at 5 cents ($.07) a cup. The !Kung are scrupulous business-women. They do not give drinks on credit, and even close kin are charged the full price for each drink. However, after the day's business is done the same women are seen sharing their wild plant foods in the traditional !Kung way with their "customers" at the evening meal.

The new !Kung culture is based on selling and drinking beer and listening (and dancing!) to hit tunes from Radio Botswana on transistor radios. !Kung drinking behavior resembles that of their Herero and Tswana neighbors, whose women also brew and sell beer. Drinking is confined to the hottest hours of the day, beginning at ten in the morning and continuing to late afternoon. The hot sun overhead must speed the alcohol's effect, because most people are thoroughly drunk by two in the afternoon. !Kung drinking parties are loud and rowdy, with shouting and laughter that can be heard a good distance away. Sometimes they take a nasty turn and fights break out, like the brawl at !Kangwa in which a mine returnee gave another man a blow with a club that fractured his skull. The situation is even worse at Chum!kwe acros the border in Namibia, where frequent injuries and even deaths occur as a result of Saturday-night (and day) brawls.

Many !Kung were appalled by the new way of life. They expressed fear at the effects of drinking on people's behavior; the loss of control, the fighting, and the neglect of daily tasks were seen as signs of the breakdown of the fabric of society. Stories were told and retold, with a mixture of glee and apprehension, of the bizarre behavior of people under the influence. A man named ≠Toma had stepped out of a drinking hut to urinate and had blithely pissed into a Herero woman's cooking pot filled with meat. In the uproar that followed he narrowly escaped a thrashing by the woman's husband. A case was brought in the headman's court, but ≠Toma disclaimed all responsibility, saying that *he* would never do such a thing; it was entirely the fault of the beer. The headman was not persuaded by this argu-ment and fined him a goat for the outrage.

Incidents like these were widely discussed and helped convince many !Kung at the other waterholes that !Kangwa was an evil place, to be avoided. The !Kung San of the interior had entered the 1960s in their isolated areas with their group structures and productive systems intact. Through the decade, the Dobe area be-came open to outside penetration, starting with the building of the Chum!kwe settlement in 1960 and continuing with the opening of the !Kangwa store and its home-brew supplies in 1967. The arrival of the anthropologists in 1963 and their continuous residence from 1967 to 1971 also had its effect. But a 1960 visitor returning in 1970 would have had no great difficulty in recognizing the !Kung he knew before. More store-bought clothes, more babies, and more donkeys and goats were in evidence, but the basic pattern remained the same. The decade of the 1970s, however, brought new challenges that threatened to change fundamentally the basic pattern of !Kung existence. The power to make decisions about their lives and future was shifting from within the community to agencies outside the Dobe area and not under their control.

THE FIRST SCHOOL

The Botswana government announced plans in 1968 to build a primary school at !Kangwa, and the school opened its doors in January 1973. The school, a two-room, single-story structure, had two teachers and offered Standards I to IV. The first class consisted of 55 Herero and Tswana students aged 5 to 10, all enrolled in Standard I. The medium of instruction was Setswana, and the curriculum was the standard one for Botswana: reading, writing, math, English, music, art, and Bible study.

Of the 60 or so !Kung children of school age, *not a single one enrolled in January 1973.* When I spoke to them in July of that year, !Kung parents claimed that the R3 ($4.50) annual school fee was too high for them. When I observed that R3 per year was not an outrageous amount for people who brewed beer and worked for wages, they responded that in addition to the fees, each child had to purchase an obligatory school outfit consisting of shoes, underpants, sweater, shirt,

The new school at !Kangwa.

and short pants for the boys, shoes, underpants, sweater, and dress for the girls, costing R15 to R17 at the local store, plus the weekly cost of the laundry soap to keep all the clothes clean. This sum put the cost of schooling out of the reach of all but a few !Kung families. For those who *could* pay for the fees and the outfits, there remained yet another problem of equal magnitude: how to feed and care for the children in !Kangwa 5 days a week for 8 months of the year. Even though the children would receive a nutritious school lunch, how was the rest of the family to forage for sufficient food in the immediate vicinity of !Kangwa, which already had a resident population of 63 !Kung? !Kung life depended on mobility, a demand that stood in direct conflict with the school's requirement of regular attendance.

!Kung parents had other objections. Especially at waterholes west and south of !Kangwa, parents expressed concern that the school was located at the village where the heaviest drinking took place. They feared their children might be beaten or neglected if they were left in the care of !Kangwa relatives. Parents also objected to the corporal punishment meted out by the schoolmaster. A fifth reason given by some parents concerned reports from relatives who had children in the school at Chum!kwe, across the border in Namibia. According to these reports, schoolchildren there were growing up to be disrespectful and contemptuous of their parents, even *zaing* them, a form of verbal sexual insulting expressly forbidden between parents and children (see Chapter 7).

In short, the !Kung were faced with a real dilemma. They had many good reasons for being suspicious of the school and its impact on their lives, yet if the children did not gain some literacy skills, they would find themselves severely disadvantaged in the rapidly evolving world of land claims, jobs, and international conflict that surrounded them. Th central government was creating laws that would increasingly have a direct impact on !Kung lives, and unless the San could read and interpret these laws and make the appropriate responses their way of life would be in danger. The ability to read and write, therefore, was becoming an even more important skill than hunting in the struggle for survival.

GOVERNMENT AND THE FUTURE OF THE SAN

Like their notions of other elements in the outside world, the !Kung ideas of government and the state were relatively hazy in 1963. *Horomenti* was their word for the government, an amalgam in their minds of Tswana and British overlords, with the British paramount. The only two individuals in high office they could name before 1963 were *Mogumagadi*, Mrs. Elizabeth Pulane, the ruling regent of the Botswana tribe and widow of the late paramount chief Moremi, and *Mosa-dinyane*, an affectionate Tswana nickname for Queen Victoria. There was some question over whether Queen Victoria and Queen Elizabeth were one and the same person. Apart from the occasional government patrols, almost the first direct contact the !Kung had with the central government was when the trucks announcing the pre-Independence elections arrived in mid-1964. I was struck by the spectacle of these "primitive" democrats being carefully instructed by means of a film on what elections were about and how to mark a ballot. !Kangwa district voted solidly for the ruling Botswana Democratic Party, the electoral symbol of which was the *Dumkra*, an automobile jack.

After Independence in 1966, their Member of the legislative assembly, Mr. Kwerepe, occasionally visited the district. From an aristocratic Tswana family, he was reputed to own *mafisa* cattle near !Kangwa. When I met him in 1967 he had just returned from a trip to the United States, where he had had lunch with Robert Kennedy. He was extolling the virtues of the American model of development through private enterprise, a model that was later put into practice in Botswana in the form of the Tribal Grazing Lands Policy (TGLP).

The TGLP provided a mechanism for taking land out of communal tenure and putting it into what amounted to freehold tenure in order to encourage more businesslike farming and ranching practices. Until Independence, the great bulk of Botswana's land had been held under a tribal form of tenure. In this system the paramount chief of each of the eight Tswana tribes doled out parcels of land to senior Tswana lineage heads to allocate grazing and agricultural rights. Effectively, it was a form of communal tenure; no land taxes or grazing fees were paid, and no one could appropriate a piece of land for his own exclusive use. In the Dobe area, this tribal tenure coexisted with the !Kung *n!ore* system: foragers and herders shared the waterholes and the space around them.

With Independence came a plan to rationalize the country's cattle industry, to take land out of tribal tenure and allocate it to individuals and syndicates on 50-year renewable leases. The lessees would survey and fence the land and would limit their herd sizes to the number of animals that could be supported in line with modern range management techniques. The plan's proponents, like Mr. Kwerepe, hailed it as the start of a new era in scientific and profitable animal production. But, like the Enclosure movement in seventeenth-century Britain and similar movements in many other Western countries, the Tribal Grazing Land Policy was a means of transforming inalienable communal land into valuable real estate, the leases for which could be bought and sold. It threatened to transform the people who lived on that land from independent hunters and herders into tenants and landless squatters.

To the government's credit, safeguards were installed to prevent the too-rapid takeover of tribal land by unscrupulous speculators. Land boards were set up in each district to screen every application before deed and title were granted. In spite of the safeguards, the !Kung of the Dobe area and other San were at a great disadvantage under the new legislation. Lacking schooling, they were quite out of their depth in the legal complexities of land board negotiations. Also, it was impossible for them to make the frequent trips to Maun to attend the land board hearings.

With the start of the 1970s, the future of the San and their role in society became a topic of discussion within the higher levels of the government. Liberal, Western-trained Batswana and expatriate civil servants saw the San, now called the *Basarwa*, as in some ways analogous to the native peoples in places like Canada

and the United States. They lived on the margins of society, were socially stigmatized, and had less opportunity for advancement than did the great majority of
their fellow citizens.

In 1974, the government established an Office for Basarwa Development
(BDO). The BDO's job was to count the Basarwa, find out what their special
needs were, and offer grants to local authorities for their welfare. In the North
West District, where Dobe was located, the !Kung received three forms of aid:
scholarships to attend primary school, aid for well-digging, and agricultural extension advice. The effects on the Dobe area were striking. By 1976–1977, over 70
!Kung children had enrolled in the two area schools, one at !Kangwa and the other
at /Xai/xai.

Craft marketing was another important development for the !Kung. For many
years the !Kung had produced some ostrich-eggshell bead necklaces for the tourist
trade. They were purchased by European traders from Ghanzi for ridiculously low
prices. Fifteen cents was paid for a string that took two days of work to produce.
The traders then resold them for ten times the amount. The government-owned
craft marketing board, Botswanacraft, was thus a boon to the !Kung and to many
other rural people. They paid the craftspeople two-thirds of retail for everything
they bought.

Income from craft production quickly rose to become the major source of cash
in the Dobe area, an influx to the community of $300 to $500 a month.

Unfortunately, the influx of cash also caused a boom in beer-making at !Kangwa,
and the practice spread to other centers. Drunkenness, squabbling, and neglect of
nutrition increased in frequency and caused a crisis in the school program. Several
parents withdrew their children from the school, fearing for the children's safety.

Well-digging was another area of emphasis by the Basarwa Development Office.
By 1977, 20 applications had been received from Dobe area !Kung for digging
permits. But here again, things didn't turn out as planned. Despite the efforts of
the BDO, 15 of the applications were tied up in red tape by local land boards, and
only 5 were approved. Of these, at only one, the well at Dobe itself, were the !Kung
successful in striking water.

The greatest successes have been recorded in agriculture and stock raising. By the
early 1980s, the number of cattle in !Kung hands had increased dramatically, and
over 50 !Kung agricultural fields had been registered with the land board. In 1980
I estimated that at least a dozen !Kung families had herds of sufficient size to
provide a substantial proportion of their diet. And six !Kung families owned steel
ploughs, a device that made agriculture possible on a greatly expanded scale.

Yet even these successes brought with them new social problems. The breakdown of sharing, the appearance for the first time of wealth differences, and a
tendency toward the subordination of women were all trends that could be discerned in embryo as the !Kung entered the last two decades of the twentieth
century.

On a recent trip to Dobe in 1980, I visited my old friend /Xashe. It was his
father, ≠Toma//gwe, who had first greeted me at Dobe Pan 17 years before
(Chapter 1). His *tsu* N!eishi had made me his "son." /Xashe's daughter //Koka,
now in her twenties, had been my "betrothed" (see Chapter 6).

The people of Dobe waterhole had prospered. We greeted with much affection, and /Xashe showed me around his new semipermanent village of well-constructed mud-walled houses that he had built with his two middle-aged brothers and an older sister. Then we visited the kraal, where I counted 19 cows and calves in the family herd, a very respectable herd size, well above the minimum for herding self-sufficiency. /Xashe and I talked over old times as his daughter //Koka, who was now happily married to a man from Chum!kwe, played her portable record player, blasting out the latest hit tunes from Johannesburg. We walked over to a smaller kraal, where his teenage son was leading 60 goats out to browse. The cows and goats of other Dobe hamlets could be heard through the trees heading out to pasture.

In a quiet glade away from the village we sat down to smoke our pipes. /Xashe, always a thoughtful person, seemed to be in an even more somber mood than usual. I asked him what was the matter.

After a long pause he replied, "It's all these people of Dobe. There are so many of them now, and all these goats, and all the cows, and all the things. And everyone has trunks full of clothes and blankets. And we argue all the time. Sometimes I wonder if we wouldn't be better off if we had stayed like we were when you first came here."

"Mi≠tum," I replied, using the term we had shared many years before, "mi≠tum, I don't know, I honestly don't know. You may be right. But whatever you and I feel, this is your life now. You can't go back."

Postscript / The !Kung of Namibia

If one could end the story here the reader might sense a happy ending of a sort. The Dobe !Kung are alive and well and holding their own in the Kalahari. But there is one more part of the story to tell. The changes that have occurred in the Dobe area, though considerable, are minimal compared to what has happened to the !Kung across the border in South-Africa-controlled Namibia, where the Marshalls made their studies and films.

In 1960 the South African government settled the Nyae Nyae !Kung at Chum!kwe (Tshum!kwi), about 35 miles west of the Botswana border. Since then the Chum!kwe !Kung have been fed, housed, missionized and schooled by the South Africans in a program of directed social change that is far more intense than anything that the Botswana government could come up with for the San in Botswana. The situation in Namibia is documented in John Marshall's film *N!ai: The Story of a !Kung Woman* (1980).

By the time of the making of the film (1978), about 900 !Kung were settled at Chum!kwe. Some of the men worked on road gangs and construction and in the station workshops; the great majority were unemployed. The women, who had almost entirely stopped their gathering activities, spent their days in household chores, visiting, and socializing, while the older children spent their days at the Chum!kwe school. Unemployment, drunkenness, and violence were increasing aspects of life at Chum!kwe through the 1970s. But the most dramatic change has been the wholesale recruitment of the !Kung into the South African army.

Since 1966 the people of Namibia have been fighting under the leadership of the South-West African People's Organization (SWAPO) to free themselves from South African illegal rule. This fight has led to the militarization of the entire northern third of the territory of Namibia. South Africa has poured men and weapons into the region and now maintains a force of 50,000 troops in Namibia. It has also made efforts to recruit soldiers locally from among the various ethnic groups, including the San. In 1974, 3–1 Battalion was organized in the Caprivi Strip north of the Dobe area, at a place called Base Omega. It now has a population of several thousand San soldiers and their dependents. From Omega the army makes regular raids into the neighboring territory of Angola.

In 1978, the war came to the interior !Kung. Battalion 3–6 was organized at Chum!kwe as a unit of South African Defense Forces. The !Kung men, attracted by the promise of high wages, joined in numbers. The !Kung troops with their families and their White officers were dispersed at small bases throughout "Bush-manland," the tiny homeland set aside for the San under South Africa's *apartheid* (racially separate development) policies. By the 1980s the !Kung units were regularly in combat, using automatic weapons and their famous tracking skills in their hunt for the "enemy." Wages of up to $500 per month were paid to the !Kung. Black Namibians from many other ethnic groups were also recruited into the South African army and were paid similar wages.

The impact of these policies on the life of the !Kung, on top of all the other changes, has been dramatic and has led to a marked deterioration in the quality of life despite the abundance of cash. As Volkman reports in *The San in Transition* (1983) (a study guide for the film *N!ai*), there has been a widespread breakdown of sharing. People used their cash income from the army and other jobs to buy great quantities of blankets and clothing, highly visible markers of new wealth and status. Others bought cattle and then slaughtered the meat and sold it to other !Kung for cash (Volkman 1983:12). This has led in turn to wealth and status differences and the emergence of new classes of rich and poor from the formerly egalitarian population. N!ai, the subject of John Marshall's film, has regularly worked as a performer in South African tourist films, and her wealth from wages is a source of resentment from her neighbors. And one !Kung man, Jo/wa Geelboi ("Yellowboy"), was given a position as a cabinet minister in the White-dominated government in the capital, Windhoek. As one observer has noted, Geelboi's home at Chum!kwe consists of a !Kung-style grass hut wrapped in a sheet. But when he is at "home" his chauffeur/bodyguard parks his new Mercedes-Benz in front of the grass hut (Volkman 1983:12).

Much of the new wealth goes into purchasing alcohol. Whereas the Dobe area !Kung have to content themselves with their home-brew (Chapter 10), the Chum!kwe !Kung can afford the best. They regularly buy beer by the case and bottles of brandy, vodka, and scotch. Drunkenness has reached alarming proportions.

The soldiers on weekend passes, armed with new weapons and a new macho image, have begun to kill each other in Saturday-night brawls. In a 35-year period, from 1920 to 1955, I recorded 22 cases of homicide (Chapter 7). In the 2 years from mid-1978 to mid-1980, 7 killings were reported at Chum!kwe alone, a rate 3 to 5 times higher than the highest levels of the earlier period.

Many of the !Kung are appalled by the violence, both external and internal. They refuse to join the army and are sympathetic to SWAPO. ≠Toma, one of the Marshalls' main informants and a former Chum!kwe headman, says in the film *N!ai*:

> SWAPO won't kill us. We're good with SWAPO and good with these soldiers, too. SWAPO will shoot the soldiers' airplanes. The soldiers will bring the fighting here. We're good people. We'd share the pot with SWAPO. But these soldiers are the owners of fighting. They fight even when they play, and I fear them. I won't let my children be soldiers, the experts at anger. The soldiers will bring the killing. This I know. (Volkman 1983:50)

Many !Kung would prefer to remain neutral, but the South African army apparently has other plans for them. John Marshall asked Captain Coetzee, the commander of the 3-6 Battalion, "What's going to happen when you go? What's going to happen to these people?"

The commander replied,

> Well, I never thought of going. I intend to stay here all my life. I can't see that we will go. And if we go, I suppose that the Bushmen will go with us. For in the Whites they find friends and they find help. They find a future living. (Volkman 1983:50)

In the last two years an interesting trend has occurred at Chum!kwe. Faced with fighting SWAPO at the army bases or with fighting each other at Chum!kwe, some people have taken a third option. Families of !Kung have been leaving the overcrowded settlement and are moving back to their traditional foraging areas like /Gausha. This "back to the bush" or "outstation" movement parallels similar movements in other parts of the foraging world. In Canada, Australia, and elsewhere in the last decades, many foraging groups have returned to the bush to recreate their life, combining traditional subsistence with regular health and other services provided by the government (see for example, Coombs *et al.* 1982).

It is too early to tell whether this experiment will be a success for the !Kung of Nyae Nyae, or what will be the final outcome of the struggle in Namibia. There is room for disagreement on both questions, and on what is the best road toward the future for the San. But whatever one's opinion, all would agree that the present situation is an extremely unhealthy one, and if left to continue unchecked could endanger the !Kung's survival. After they survived in the Kalahari for so many centuries, is this now to be the fate of the Namibian !Kung?

Happily, the pace of life in Botswana is moving more slowly, and this gives the !Kung there some breathing space. Botswana's limited resources do not permit its government to pour money into the Dobe area on the scale of the Chum!kwe settlement, and this may be a blessing in disguise. The government and people of Botswana, like most of the peoples of Africa, are sympathetic to SWAPO and hope to see a SWAPO government eventually in power in Namibia. When a number of Botswana !Kung, attracted by the high wages, tried to cross the border to join the South African forces, the government put a stop to it and passed a law forbidding foreign enlistment. As a result, the Dobe !Kung have largely stayed out of the conflict in Namibia, and though contact and intermarriage is frequent between Dobe and Chum!kwe, the Dobe !Kung have continued to move ahead at their own pace.

The evidence for homicide and the general level of violence among the !Kung both in the early and the recent period should dispel once and for all the image of the !Kung as shy and gentle or unable to defend themselves. It is inevitable that with this revised view of the !Kung, they will be compared or contrasted with the Yanomamö, described in another case study in this series (Chagnon 1983). The Yanomamö, horticulturalists in the interior of Venezuela, are far more violent than the !Kung. Warfare and mock duels are a constant fact of Yanomamö life; both were absent (until recently) among the !Kung. Both the Yanomamö and the !Kung have been proposed at times as being typical of our ancestors, the prototype of "early man." Chagnon himself at one point called the Yanomamö "our contemporary ancestors" (1977:164), and he further implied that Yanomamö aggressiveness was typical of ancestral humans. This kind of image for either people is one that we must treat with extreme caution. The Yanomamö, though fierce, are not even foragers. They are farmers who hunt, and the bulk of their diet comes from their cultivated fields. This way of life is at most only a few thousand years old. Hunting and gathering as a human adaptation, by contrast, is at least 100 times older. The !Kung *are* hunter-gatherers and have been, so far as we can tell, for thousands of years, but even they have lived for centuries in a world of nonhunting peoples.

But the most telling criticism of the view that simple societies are inherently aggressive comes from the fact that violence and aggression, far from being a constant, are among the most variable aspects of human life. The Namibian !Kung illustrate this point. If you visited the Nyae Nyae !Kung in 1950, you would say they were relatively peaceful. If you visited them 30 years later at Chum!kwe, you would say they were among the most violent people on earth. In the space of a few short years their whole attitude towards violence has been transformed, and their homicide rate has tripled. Given this variability, in what sense can we say that the !Kung are inherently aggressive? We don't have this kind of before-after case study for the Yanomamö, but it is worth mentioning that Chagnon's study focuses on only one population of the Yanomamö-speaking peoples, a segment that happened to be very warlike. It may surprise the reader that, as Harris points out, the majority of the Yanomamö lead far more peaceful lives, living on riverine resources elsewhere in Venezuela and Brazil (Harris 1977:47–54).

It is clear that neither the !Kung nor the Yanomamö can be taken as typical of our hunting and gathering ancestors. The Yanomamö aren't even foragers, and each people has its own history, politics, and adaptation to environment. If anything unites these two famous peoples, it is that both are facing the end of their independence and way of life as a result of contact with a powerful outside force: the Western world. These threats to their existence are what we should be studying in earnest, and not the dubious claims that either represents our ancestors, or exemplifies human nature in the raw.

Appendix / Eating Christmas in the Kalahari[1]

The !Kung knowledge of Christmas is thirdhand. The London Missionary Society brought the holiday to the southern Tswana tribes in the early nineteenth century. Later, native catechists spread the idea far and wide among the Bantu-speaking pastoralists, even in the remotest corners of the Kalahari Desert. The !Kung idea of the Christmas story, stripped to its essentials, is "praise the birth of White Man's god-chief"; what keeps their interest in the holiday high is the Tswana-Herero custom of slaughtering an ox for their !Kung neighbors as an annual goodwill gesture. Since the 1930s, part of the San's annual round of activities has included a December congregation at the cattle posts for trading, marriage brokering, and several days of trance-dance feasting at which the local Tswana headman is host.

As a social anthropologist working with the !Kung, I found that the Christmas ox custom suited my purposes. I had come to the Kalahari to study the hunting and gathering subsistence economy of the !Kung, and to accomplish this it was essential not to provide them with food, share my own food, or interfere in any way with their food-gathering activities. While liberal handouts of tobacco and medical supplies were appreciated, they were scarcely adequate to erase the glaring disparity in wealth between the anthropologist, who maintained a two-month inventory of canned goods, and the !Kung, who rarely had a day's supply of food on hand. My approach, while paying off in terms of data, left me open to frequent accusations of stinginess and hard-heartedness. By their lights, I was a miser.

The Christmas ox was to be my way of saying thank you for the cooperation of the past year; and since it was to be our last Christmas in the field, I determined to slaughter the largest, meatiest ox that money could buy, insuring that the feast and trance dance would be a success.

Through December I kept my eyes open at the wells as the cattle were brought down for watering. Several animals were offered, but none had quite the grossness that I had in mind. Then, ten days before the holiday, a Herero friend led an ox of astonishing size and mass up to our camp. It was solid black, stood five feet high at the shoulder, had a five-foot span of horns, and must have weighed 1200 pounds on the hoof. Food consumption calculations are my specialty, and I quickly figured that bones and viscera aside, there was enough meat—at least four pounds—

---

[1] From "Eating Christmas in the Kalahari," by Richard Borshay Lee, with permission from *Natural History*, December, 1969; Copyright the American Museum of Natural History, 1969.

for every man, woman, and child of the 150 !Kung in the vicinity of /Xai/xai who were expected at the feast.

Having found the right animal at last, I paid the Herero £20 ($56) and asked him to keep the beast with his herd until Christmas day. The next morning word spread among the people that the big solid-black one was the ox chosen by /Tontah for the Christmas feast. That afternoon I received the first delegation. Ben!a, an outspoken 60-year-old mother of five, came to the point slowly.

"Where were you planning to eat Christmas?"

"Right here at /Xai/xai," I replied.

"Alone or with others?"

"I expect to invite all the people to eat Christmas with me."

"Eat what?"

"I have purchased Yehave's black ox, and I am going to slaughter and cook it."

"That's what we were told at the well but refused to believe it until we heard it from yourself."

"Well, it's the black one," I replied expansively, although wondering what she was driving at.

"Oh, no!" Ben!a groaned, turning to her group. "They were right." Turning back to me she asked, "Do you expect us to eat that bag of bones?"

"Bag of bones! It's the biggest ox at /Xai/xai."

"Big, yes, but old. And thin. Everybody knows there's no meat on that old ox. What did you expect us to eat off it, the horns?"

Everybody chuckled at Ben!a's one-liner as they walked away, but all I could manage was a weak grin.

That evening it was the turn of the young men. They came to sit at our evening fire. /Gaugo, about my age, spoke to me man-to-man.

"/Tontah, you have always been square with us. What has happened to change your heart? That sack of guts and bones of Yehave's will hardly feed one camp, let alone all the !Kung around /Xai/xai." And he proceeded to enumerate the seven camps in the /Xai/xai vicinity, family by family. "Perhaps you have forgotten that we are not few, but many. Or are you too blind to tell the difference between a proper cow and an old wreck? That ox is thin to the point of death."

"Look, you guys," I retorted, "that is a beautiful animal, and I'm sure you will eat it with pleasure at Christmas."

"Of course we will eat it; it's food. But it won't fill us up to the point where we will have enough strength to dance. We will eat and go home to bed with stomachs rumbling."

That night as we turned in, I asked my wife Nancy: "What did you think of the black ox?"

"It looked enormous to me. Why?"

"Well, about eight different people have told me I got gypped; that the ox is nothing but bones."

"What's the angle?" Nancy asked. "Did they have a better one to sell?"

"No, they just said that it was going to be a grim Christmas because there won't be enough meat to go around. Maybe I'll get an independent judge to look at the beast in the morning."

Bright and early, Halingisi, a Tswana cattleowner, appeared at our camp. But before I could ask him to give me his opinion on Yehave's black ox, he gave me the eye signal that indicated a confidential chat. We left the camp and sat down.

"/Tontah, I'm surprised at you; you've lived here for three years and still haven't learned anything about cattle."

"But what else can a person do but choose the biggest, strongest animal one can find?" I retorted.

"Look, just because an animal is big doesn't mean that it has plenty of meat on it. The black one was a beauty when it was younger, but now it is thin to the point of death."

"Well, I've already bought it. What can I do at this stage?"

"Bought it already? I thought you were just considering it. Well, you'll have to kill it and serve it, I suppose. But don't expect much of a dance to follow."

My spirits dropped rapidly. I could believe that Ben!a and /Gaugo just might be putting me on about the black ox, but Halingisi seemed to be an impartial critic. I went around that day feeling as though I had bought a lemon of a used car.

In the afternoon it was Tomazo's turn. Tomazo is a fine hunter, a top trance performer, and one of my most reliable informants. He approached the subject of the Christmas cow as part of my continuing education.

"My friend, the way it is with us !Kung," he began, "is that we love meat. And even more than that, we love fat. When we hunt we always search for the fat ones, the ones dripping with layers of white fat: fat that turns into a clear, thick oil in the cooking pot, fat that slides down your gullet, fills your stomach and gives you a roaring diarrhea," he rhapsodized.

"So, feeling as we do," he continued, "it gives us pain to be served such a scrawny thing as Yehave's black ox. It is big, yes, and no doubt its giant bones are good for soup, but fat it what we really crave, and so we will eat Christmas this year with a heavy heart."

The prospect of a gloomy Christmas now had me worried, so I asked Tomazo what I could do about it.

"Look for a fat one, a young one . . . smaller, but fat. Fat enough to make us //gom ('evacuate the bowels'); then we will be happy."

My suspicions were aroused when Tomazo said that he happened to know of a young, fat, barren cow that the owner was willing to part with. Was Tomazo working on commission, I wondered? But I dispelled this unworthy thought when we approached the Herero owner of the cow in question and found that he had decided not to sell.

The scrawny wreck of a Christmas ox now became the talk of the /Xai/xai waterhole and was the first news told to the outlying groups as they began to come in from the bush for the feast. What finally convinced me that real trouble might be brewing was the visit from /N!au, an old conservative with a reputation for fierceness. His nickname meant spear and referred to an incident thirty years ago in which he had speared a man to death. He had an intense manner; fixing me with his eyes, he said in clipped tones:

"I have only just heard about the black ox today, or else I would have come here earlier. /Tontah, do you honestly think you can serve meat like that to people and avoid a fight?" He paused, letting the implications sink in. "I don't mean fight you, /Tontah; you are a White man. I mean a fight between !Kung. There are many fierce ones here, and with such a small quantity of meat to distribute, how can you give everybody a fair share? Someone is sure to accuse another of taking too much or hogging all the choice pieces. Then you will see what happens when some go hungry while others eat."

The possibility of at least a serious argument struck me as all too real. I had witnessed the tension that surrounds the distribution of meat from a kudu or gemsbok kill, and had documented many arguments that sprang up from a real or imagined slight in meat distribution. The owners of a kill may spend up to two hours arranging and rearranging the piles of meat under the gaze of a circle of recipients before handing them out. And I also knew that the Christmas feast at /Xai/xai would be bringing together groups that had feuded in the past.

Convinced now of the gravity of the situation, I went in earnest to search for a second cow; but all my inquiries failed to turn one up.

The Christmas feast was evidently going to be a disaster, and the incessant complaints about the meagerness of the ox had already taken the fun out of it for me. Moreover, I was getting bored with the wisecracks, and after losing my temper a few times, I resolved to serve the beast anyway. If the meat fell short, the hell with it. In the !Kung idiom, I announced to all who would listen:

"I am a poor man and blind. If I have chosen one that is too old and too thin, we will eat it anyway and see if there is enough meat there to quiet the rumbling of our stomachs."

On hearing this speech, Ben!a offered me a rare word of comfort. "It's thin," she said philosophically, "but the bones will make a good soup."

At dawn Christmas morning, instinct told me to turn over the butchering and cooking to a friend and take off with Nancy and spend Christmas alone in the bush. But curiosity kept me from retreating. I wanted to see what such a scrawny ox looked like on butchering, and if there *was* going to be a fight, I wanted to catch every word of it. Anthropologists are incurable that way.

The great beast was driven up to our dancing ground, and a shot in the forehead dropped it in its tracks. Then, freshly cut branches were heaped around the fallen carcass to receive the meat. Ten men volunteered to help with the cutting. I asked /Gaugo to make the breast bone cut. This cut, which begins the butchering process for most large game, offers easy access for removal of the viscera. But it also allows the hunter to spot-check the amount of fat on the animal. A fat game animal carries a white layer up to an inch thick on the chest, while in a thin one, the knife will quickly cut to bone. All eyes fixed on his hand as /Gaugo, dwarfed by the great carcass, knelt to the breast. The first cut opened a pool of solid white in the black skin. The second and third cut widened and deepened the creamy white. Still no bone. It was pure fat; it must have been two inches thick.

"Hey /Gau," I burst out, "that ox is loaded with fat. What's this about the ox being too thin to bother eating? Are you out of your mind?"

"Fat?" /Gau shot back, "You call that fat? This wreck is thin, sick, dead!" And he broke out laughing. So did everyone else. They rolled on the ground, paralyzed with laughter. Everybody laughed except me; I was thinking.

I ran back to the tent and burst in just as Nancy was getting up. "Hey, the black ox. It's fat as hell! They were kidding about it being too thin to eat. It was a joke or something. A put-on. Everyone is really delighted with it!"

"Some joke," my wife replied. "It was so funny that you were ready to pack up and leave /Xai/xai."

If it had indeed been a joke, it had been an extraordinarily convincing one, and tinged, I thought, with more than a touch of malice, as many jokes are. Nevertheless, that it was a joke lifted my spirits considerably, and I returned to the butchering site, where the shape of the ox was rapidly disappearing under the axes and knives of the butchers. The atmosphere had become festive. Grinning broadly, their arms covered with blood well past the elbow, men packed chunks of meat into the big cast-iron cooking pots, 50 pounds to the load, and muttered and chuckled all the while about the thinness and worthlessness of the animal and /Tontah's poor judgment.

We danced and ate that ox for two days and two nights; we cooked and distributed 14 potfuls of meat, and no one went home hungry and no fights broke out.

But the "joke" stayed in my mind. I had a growing feeling that something important had happened in my relationship with the !Kung, and that the clue lay in the meaning of the joke. Several days later, when most of the people had dispersed back to the bush camps, I raised the question with Hakekgose, a Tswana man who had grown up among the !Kung, married a !Kung girl, and who probably knew their culture better than any other non-!Kung.

"With us Whites," I began, "Christmas is supposed to be the day of friendship and brotherly love. What I can't figure out is why the !Kung went to such lengths to criticize and belittle the ox I had bought for the feast. The animal was perfectly good, and their jokes and wisecracks practically ruined the holiday for me."

"So it really did bother you," said Hakekgose. "Well, that's the way they always talk. When I take my rifle and go hunting with them, if I miss, they laugh at me for the rest of the day. But even if I hit and bring one down, it's no better. To them, the kill is always too small or too old or too thin; and as we sit down on the kill site to cook and eat the liver, they keep grumbling, even with their mouths full of meat. They say things like, 'Oh this is awful! What a worthless animal! Whatever made me think that this Tswana rascal could hunt!' "

"Is this the way outsiders are treated?" I asked.

"No, it is their custom; they talk that way to each other too. Go and ask them."

/Gaugo had been one of the most enthusiastic in making me feel bad about the merit of the Christmas ox. I sought him out first.

"Why did you tell me the black ox was worthless, when you could see that it was loaded with fat and meat?"

"Is it our way," he said, smiling. "We always like to fool people about that. Say there is a !Kung who has been hunting. He must not come home and announce like a braggart, 'I have killed a big one in the bush!' He must first sit down in silence until I or someone else comes up to his fire and asks, 'What did you see today?' He replies quietly, 'Ah, I'm no good for hunting. I saw nothing at all [pause] just a little tiny one.' Then I smile to myself," /Gaugo continued, "because I know he has killed something big.

"In the morning we make up a party of four or five people to cut up and carry the meat back to the camp. When we arrive at the kill we examine it and cry out, 'You mean to say you have dragged us all the way out here in order to make us cart home your pile of bones? Oh, if I had known it was this thin I wouldn't have come.' Another one pipes up, 'People, to think I gave up a nice day in the shade for this. At home we may be hungry, but at least we have nice cool water to drink.' If the horns are big, someone says, 'Did you think that somehow you were going to boil down the horns for soup?'

"To all this you must respond in kind. 'I agree,' you say, 'this one is not worth the effort; let's just cook the liver for strength and leave the rest for the hyenas. It is not too late to hunt today, and even a duiker or a steenbok would be better than this mess.'

"Then you set to work nevertheless, butcher the animal, carry the meat back to the camp, and everyone eats," /Gaugo concluded.

Things were beginning to make sense. Next, I went to Tomazo. He corroborated /Gaugo's story of the obligatory insults over a kill and added a few details of his own.

"But," I asked, "why insult a man after he has gone to all that trouble to track and kill an animal and when he is going to share the meat with you so that your children will have something to eat?"

"Arrogance," was his cryptic answer.

"Arrogance?"

"Yes, when a young man kills much meat he comes to think of himself as a chief or a big man, and he thinks of the rest of us as his servants or inferiors. We can't accept this. We refuse one who boasts, for someday his pride will make him kill somebody. So he always speak of his meat as worthless. This way we cool his heart and make him gentle."

"But why didn't you tell me this before?" I asked Tomazo with some heat.

"Because you never asked me," said Tomazo, echoing the refrain that has come to haunt every field ethnographer.

The pieces now fell into place. I had known for a long time that in situations of social conflict with !Kung I held all the cards. I was the only source of tobacco in a thousand square miles, and I was not incapable of cutting an individual off for noncooperation. Though my boycott never lasted longer than a few days, it was an indication of my strength. People resented my presence at the waterhole, yet simultaneously dreaded my leaving. In short, I was a perfect target for the charge of arrogance and for the !Kung tactic of enforcing humility.

I had been taught an object lesson by the !Kung; it had come from an unexpected corner and had hurt me in a vulnerable area. For the big black ox was to be the one totally generous, unstinting act of my year at /Xai/xai, and I was quite unprepared for the reaction I received.

As I read it, their message was this: There are no totally generous acts. All "acts" have an element of calculation. One black ox slaughtered at Christmas does not wipe out a year of careful manipulation of gifts given to serve your own ends. After all, to kill an animal and share the meat with people is really no more than !Kung do for each other every day and with far less fanfare.

In the end, I had to admire how the !Kung had played out the farce—collectively straight-faced to the end. Curiously, the episode reminded me of the *Good Soldier Schweik* and his marvelous encounters with authority. Like Schweik, the !Kung had retained a thoroughgoing skepticism of good intentions. Was it this independence of spirit, I wondered, that had kept them culturally viable in the face of generations of contact with more powerful societies, both Black and White? The thought that the !Kung were alive and well in the Kalahari was strangely comforting. Perhaps, armed with that independence and with their superb knowledge of their environment, they might yet survive the future.

Glossary of !Kung and other non-English terms

Basarwa (sarwa):   the Setswana term for San; includes the !Kung and a number of other San peoples.
bogadi: bride price in Setswana.
chuana: the !Kung leather breechclout.
chu/o: a camp or village.
//gangwa: God.
//gangwasi: ghosts of the dead.
hxaro: traditional system of delayed reciprocal exchange.
kamasi: gifts exchanged between a prospective groom and his future wife's parents.
kaross: a leather garment and carrying device worn by women.
k"ausi: owners.
kgotla: the Tswana court of law.
!kia: the trance state of the healers.
kraal: corral, an enclosure for keeping cattle and goats.
!kun!a: old name, used for someone with the same name as oneself (man speaking).
mafisa: cattle lent out by Tswana on a sharecropping basis.
molapo: a dry river course.
mongongo: a fruit and nut, the main food of the Dobe !Kung (*Ricinodendron rautanenii*).
n/um: medicine, energy, power, anything strange or extraordinary.
n/um k"au: owner of *n/um*, a healer.
n≠amasi: roads or paths along which *hxaro* goods travel.
n!ore: an area of land held by a !Kung camp.
swara: the kin term for brother-in-law when members of two different ethnic groups marry.
t'si: the bush, wilderness.
wi: to help, to be older than, important in determining kinship.
za: to sexually insult.
zhu/twasi: "genuine people," the !Kung term for themselves.
≠tum: father-in-law, son-in-law.

Films on the !Kung:
an annotated list

Many high-quality films are available on the !Kung, making them one of the best-documented foraging peoples on film. Films marked with an asterick* have an accompanying study guide. Except where noted, all films are in color. Particularly relevant films are keyed into appropriate chapters in this book.

Films by John Marshall

These excellent films are based on footage shot by John Marshall in the 1950s. They are widely available in film libraries throughout North America. They may also be rented or purchased from:

Documentary Educational Resources
Dept. TDK
5 Bridge Street
Watertown, Mass. 02172
[617–926–0491]

*_Argument about a Marriage_. 19 min. Conflict between two !Kung bands concerning the legitimacy of a marriage. Dramatically illustrates how conflicts flare up to the threshold of violence.

(Chapters 6 and 7)

*_Baobab Play_. 8 min. A group of children and teenagers throw toy spears into a tree, trying to make them stick into the bark. Accompanied by 8 pages of film notes.

*_Bitter Melons_. 28–½ min. Music of the /Gwi San musician and composer, Ukxone, illustrated with documentary material. Animal songs and games are played together with songs of the land that the /Gwi people depend on for their livelihood and social life. (Reviewed by Alan Lomax, _American Anthropologist_ 74:1018–1020, 1972.)

(Chapters 2–4)

A Curing Ceremony. 8 min. (b&w) Sa//gai, a young woman about to have a miscarriage, is cured by /Ti!kay, who enters a mild trance without the stimulus of dancing. (Reviewed by Nancie L. Gonzalez et al., _American Anthropologist_ 77:175, 1975.)

(Chapter 8)

161

Debe's Tantrum. 8–½ min. Di!ai has planned to gather sweet berries with her sister and to leave her five-year-old son, Debe, behind with his half-sister, N!ai. Debe, looking forward to the trip, strongly resists being left. The predicament becomes hopeless and Di!ai struggles off, bearing Debe on her back.

A Group of Women. 5 min. (b&w). !Kung women resting, talking, and nursing a baby while lying under the shade of a baobab tree.

The Hunters. 73 min. Life and culture of a group of !Kung Bushmen in the northern Kalahari Desert, emphasizing the quest for food in the harsh environment. The climax of the film is the epic chase after a giraffe is wounded by a poison arrow. Overemphasizes the dramatic at the expense of the routine and secure nature of !Kung subsistence.

(Chapter 4)

A Joking Relationship. 12–½ min. (b&w). For the !Kung, the joking relationship provides opportunities for emotional support. It is an important part of kinship behavior. This film depicts a moment of flirtation in a joking relationship between N!ai, the young wife of /Tontah, and her great-uncle /Ti!kay. N!ai, as an adult, is featured in John Marshall's recent film *N!ai: The Story of a !Kung Woman.*

(Chapter 5)

!Kung Bushmen Hunting Equipment. 37 min.

(Chapter 4)

*Lion Game. 3–½ min. /Tontah, a young man, plays a lion and is "hunted" and "killed" by a group of boys.

(Chapter 4)

*The Meat Fight. 14 min. An argument arises between two camps when an antelope killed by a hunter from one band is found and distributed by a man from another band. *The Meat Fight* illustrates dramatically the social structure of conflict and the role of leaders in !Kung society. Accompanied by a 28-page Study Guide.

(Chapters 4 and 7)

Men Bathing. 14 min. In Nyae Nyae, if the rains have been heavy, water will stay in open pans, like small lakes, all year. One morning five !Kung men went to Nama pan. /Ti!kay came to wash the clothes he had acquired on his trip to rescue his wives from White farmers. The other men came to bathe. The men use the opportunity to launch sexual jokes at each other.

(Chapter 5)

N!owa T'ama: The Melon Tossing Game. 14–½ min. The melon tossing game is unique in the complexity and stability of its music and in the frequency with which it is played. In this film, women and girls from three separate !Kung bands have gathered at a mongongo grove to play a long and intense game in which undertones of social and personal tension become apparent.

*N/um Tchai. 20 min. (b&w). An excellent introduction to *n/um* and the !Kung healing dance. At a dawn healing dance a young trance performer named /Tontah experiences the violent onset of *!kia.* He is helped through the difficult transition by his teacher and other men.

(Chapter 8)

Playing with Scorpions. 4 min. !Kung people, by and large, are not excited by the threat of dangerous encounters with each other or their environment. But !Kung children, tempting fate in small ways, sometimes play with scorpions.

(Chapters 3 and 4)

**A Rite of Passage.* 14 min. Hunting has a special importance among the !Kung. The people crave meat; they need skins for clothing and sacks, and sinews to make string for bows and nets. The importance of hunting is symbolized in a small ceremony that takes place when a boy has killed his first antelope. The film depicts such a ceremony from the time /Ti!kay, a young boy, shoots his first wildebeeste, through the tracking and finding of the animal, the cooking and eating of the meat, and the symbolic scarification.

(Chapter 4)

**Tug of War.* 6 min. Twelve or more boys, in two teams, wrestle over a length of rubber hose. Accompanied by 6 pages of film notes.

**The Wasp Nest.* 20 min. Gathering wild foods is a basic subsistence activity and is the responsibility of women. This film follows a group of women and children as they gather sweet, fresh ≠oley berries and *sha* roots.

(Chapter 4)

The next film was made by John Marshall for the Odyssey Television Series in 1978 and released in 1980.

**N!ai: The Story of a !Kung Woman.* 53 min. This powerful film is an update on the state of the !Kung 25 years after the Marshalls' first visits. We follow N!ai's life through flashbacks from her hunting and gathering childhood to her contemporary life on a South African settlement station in Namibia. The impact of the cash economy, schools, missionaries, and the recruitment of the San into the South African army are brilliantly explored in this important documentary. A 56-page study guide entitled *The San in Transition*, by Toby A. Volkman, was issued in 1983.

(Chapter 10 and Postscript)

Other Films

Bushmen of the Kalahari. 12 min. Focuses upon the /Gwi San of the central Kalahari Desert of Botswana. Narrated by Dr. George Silberbauer, the film becomes an implied question: "What is Civilization?" /Gwi live in a harmonious self-contained community whose existence is dependent upon women finding roots and men tracking and killing game with bow and arrows. Silberbauer speculates on the Bushman's future as technological society moves closer and closer to his boundaries. (Reviewed by John Marshall, *American Anthropologist* 73:502–503, 1971.)

Bushmen of the Kalahari: Parts 1 and 2 (1975). 50 min. National Geographic Society. Filmmaker-anthropologist John Marshall revisits the same !Kung Bushmen he filmed fifteen years earlier. During the years, the !Kung people have changed their subsistence from gathering-hunting to a reliance on water pumps, goats, horses, and work as ranch hands. Though technically sound, the film suffers from a contrived plot line imposed by the National Geographic producers. *N!ai* (see above) is a much better film.

A Human Way of Life. Part 2/3 of the series *The Making of Mankind.* 50
minutes. Hosted by Richard Leakey and featuring Richard Lee, this 1980
BBC film is the only film that has been made specifically about the !Kung of
the Dobe area. Filmed mainly at Dobe waterhole, it illustrates graphically
the main points covered in this book: the security of subsistence, the skill
of the hunters, the rich social life, and relations between men and women. The
film features many of the Dobe people whose words appear in this book.
[Note that the film also highlights the archeological studies of Glynn Isaac in
Kenya.] Available for rental or purchase in 16mm or video cassette from:

> Time-Life Video Dept. TDK (Part 2)
> P.O. Box 644
> Paramus, N.J. 07652

In Canada:

> British Broadcasting Corp. (Part 3)
> 55 Bloor St. W., Suite 1220
> Toronto, Canada M4W 1A5

or at BBC offices abroad.

(all chapters)

References cited and recommended readings*

Barnard, Alan. 1976. Nharo Bushman kinship and the transformation of Khoi kin categories. Unpublished Ph.D. thesis. University of London.

Barnard, Alan. 1978. Universal systems of kin categorization. *African Studies* 37(1):69–81.

Biesele, Megan. 1976. Aspects of !Kung folklore. In R. B. Lee and Irven DeVore, eds., *Kalahari Hunter-Gatherers* (Cambridge, Mass.: Harvard University Press), pp. 302–324.

Bleek, Dorothea. 1928. *The Naron: A Bushman Tribe of the Kalahari*. Cambridge: Cambridge University Press.

Brooks, Allison, and John Yellen. 1979. Archaeological excavations at ≠Gi: A preliminary report on the first two field sessions. *Botswana Notes and Records* 9:21–30.

Brooks, Allison, Diane E. Gelburd, and John Yellen. 1981. Food production and culture change among the !Kung San: Implications for prehistoric research. In J. Clark and S. Brandt, eds., *Causes and Consequences of Food Productions in Africa* (Berkeley: University of California Press).

Cashdon, Elizabeth. 1977. Subsistence, mobility, and territories among the G//anakwe of the northeastern Central Kalahari Game Reserve. Mimeograph Report to the Ministry of Local Government and Lands, Gaborone, Botswana.

Chagnon, Napoleon. 1983. *Yanomamö: The Fierce People*, 3d ed. New York: Holt, Rinehart and Winston: Case Studies in Cultural Anthropology.

Chapman, Thomas. 1868. *Travels in the Interior of South Africa*. London: Bell and Daldy.

Coombs, H. C., B. G. Dexter, and L. R. Hiatt. 1982. The outstation movement in aboriginal Australia. In E. Leacock and R. Lee, eds., *Politics and History in Band Societies* (Cambridge: Cambridge University Press), pp. 427–440.

Darwin, Charles. 1958 (orig. 1859). *The Origin of Species*. New York: New American Library, Mentor.

Eibl-Eibesfeldt, I. 1972. *Die !Ko-Buschmanngesellschaft: Gruppenbindung und Aggressions-Kontrolle*. Munich: Piper.

Fabian, J. 1965. !Kung Bushman Kinship: Componential Analysis and Alternative Interpretations. *Anthropos* 60:663–718.

Fourie, L. M. 1928. The Bushmen of South West Africa. In C. Hahn, H. Vedder, and L. Fourie, eds., *The Native Tribes of South West Africa* (New York: Barnes and Noble), pp. 79–106.

Guenther, Mathias. 1979. *The Farm Bushmen of the Ghanzi District Botswana*. Stuttgart: Hochschul Verlag.

Harris, Marvin. 1977. *Cannibals and Kings: The Origins of Cultures*. New York: Random House.

* Readings marked with an asterisk are especially recommended for further study.

Heinz, H. J. 1966. Social organization of the !Ko Bushmen. Master's thesis. Department of Anthropology, University of South Africa, Pretoria.

Heinz, H. J. 1972. Territoriality among the Bushmen in general and the !Ko in particular. *Anthropos* 67:405–416.

Hitchcock, Robert. 1982. Patterns of sedentism among the Basarwa of eastern Botswana. In E. Leacock and R. Lee, eds., *Politics and History in Band Societies* (Cambridge: Cambridge University Press), pp. 223–267.

*Howell, Nancy. 1979. *Demography of the Dobe !Kung.* New York: Academic Press.

*Katz, Richard. 1982. *Boiling Energy: Community Healing among the Kalahari !Kung.* Cambridge, Mass.: Harvard University Press.

*Leacock, Eleanor, and Richard Lee, eds., 1982 *Politics and History in Band Societies.* Cambridge: Cambridge University Press.

Lee, Richard B. 1967. Trance cure of the !Kung Bushmen. *Natural History* (November):30–37.

*Lee, Richard B. 1979. *The !Kung San: Men, Women, and Work in a Foraging* perspective. *Human Ecology* 1(2):125–47.

Lee, Richard B. 1975. The !Kungs' new culture. In *Science Year 1976* (Chicago: World Book Encyclopedia), pp. 180–195.

*Lee, Richard B. 1979. *The !Kung San: Men, Women and Work in a Foraging Society.* Cambridge: Cambridge University Press.

Lee, Richard B., and Irven DeVore, eds., 1968. *Man the Hunter.* Chicago: Aldine.

*Lee, Richard B., and Irven DeVore, eds., 1976. *Kalahari Hunter-Gatherers: Studies of the !Kung San and their Neighbors.* Cambridge, Mass.: Harvard University Press.

*Lewis-Williams, D. 1981. *Believing and Seeing: Symbolic Meanings in Southern San Rock Paintings.* New York: Academic Press.

*Marshall, John. 1980. *N!ai: The Story of a !Kung Woman* (see Film Guide). Watertown, Mass.: Documentary Educational Resources.

Marshall, Lorna. 1957. The kin terminology system of the !Kung Bushmen. *Africa* 27:1–25.

Marshall, Lorna. 1960. !Kung Bushmen Bands. *Africa* 30:325–355.

Marshall, Lorna. 1962. !Kung Bushman religious beliefs. *Africa* 32(3):221–225.

Marshall, Lorna. 1969. The medicine dance of the !Kung Bushmen. *Africa* 39(4): 347–381.

*Marshall, Lorna. 1976. *The !Kung of Nyae Nyae.* Cambridge, Mass.: Harvard University Press.

Meissner, M., et al. 1975. No exit for wives: Sexual division of labour and the cumulation of household demands. *Canadian Review of Sociology and Anthropology* 12(4):424–439.

Radcliffe-Brown, A. R. 1930. The social organization of Australian tribes. Part 1. *Oceania* 1:34–63.

Sbrzesny, H. 1976. *Die Spiele der !Ko-Buschleute.* Munich: Piper.

Schapera, Isaac. 1930. *The Khoisan People of South Africa: Bushmen and Hottentots.* London: Routledge and Kegan Paul.

Shostak, Marjorie. 1976. A !Kung woman's memories of childhood. In R. Lee and I. DeVore, eds., *Kalahari Hunter-Gatherers* (Cambridge, Mass.: Harvard University Press), pp. 246–277.

Shostak, Marjorie. 1981. *Nisa: The Life and Words of a !Kung Woman.* Cambridge, Mass.: Harvard University Press.

*Shostak, Marjorie. 1983. *Nisa: The Life and Words of a !Kung Woman.* New York: Vintage Books.

Silberbauer, George. 1965. *Bushman Survey Report.* Gaborone: Bechuanaland Government.

*Silberbauer, George. 1981. *Hunter and Habitat in the Central Kalahari Desert.* Cambridge: Cambridge University Press.

Sillery, Anthony. 1952. *The Bechuanaland Protectorate.* Cape Town: Oxford University Press.

Tanaka, Jiro. (Translated by David W. Hughes.) 1980. *The San, Hunter-Gatherers of the Kalahari: A Study in Ecological Anthropology.* Tokyo: University of Tokyo Press.

*Thomas, Elizabeth Marshall. 1959. *The Harmless People.* New York: Knopf.

Traill, Tony. 1974. *The Compleat Guide to the Koon.* African Studies Institute Communication, No. 2, pp. 1–102. Johannesburg: University of the Witwatersrand.

Vierich, Helga. 1982. Adaptive flexibility in a multi-ethnic setting: the Basarwa of the Southern Kalahari. In E. Leacock and R. Lee, eds., *Politics and History in Band Societies* (Cambridge: Cambridge University Press), pp. 213–222.

*Volkman, Toby A. 1983. *The San in Transition: Volume I, A Guide to "N!ai: The Story of a !Kung Woman."* Cambridge, Mass.: Documentary Educational Resources (D.E.R.) and Cultural Survival.

Wiessner, Pauline. 1977. *Hxaro*: A regional system of reciprocity for the !Kung San. Ph.D. Dissertation, University of Michigan, Ann Arbor.

Weissner, Pauline. 1982. Risk, reciprocity and social influences in !Kung San economics. In E. Leacock and R. Lee, eds., *Politics and History in Band Societies* (Cambridge: Cambridge University Press), pp. 61–84.

Wilmsen, Edwin. 1978. Seasonal effects of dietary intake on Kalahari San. *Federation of American Societies for Experimental Biology Proceedings* 37(1): 65–72.

Wilmsen, Edwin. 1981. Exchange, interaction and settlement in North Western Botswana: Past and present perspectives. *Working Paper No. 39*, African Studies Center, Boston University.

Winterhalder, Bruce, and Eric A. Smith, eds., 1981. *Optional Foraging Strategies.* Chicago: University of Chicago Press.

Wolf, Eric R. 1982. *Europe and the People without History.* Berkeley and Los Angeles: University of California Press.

Woodburn, James. 1982. Social dimensions of death in four African hunting and gathering societies. In M. Block and J. Parry, eds., *Death and the Regeneration of Life* (London: Athlone), pp. 187–210.

Yellen, John. 1977. *Archeological Approaches to the Present: Models for Reconstructing the Past.* New York: Academic Press.

Index

Adaptation, mobility as essence of, 29, 39

Affines, and avoidance relationships, 65, 66, 126; and Black-!Kung marriages, 126–128; and food security, 82; and gift exchange, 82, 83, 98; kin terms for, 65–66, 126–128

Age, at marriage, 74, 76–77; relative, and kin terms, 63, 70; and status distinctions, 63, 70

Aggression, and view of simple societies, 149–150

See also Conflict; Fighting; Homicide; Violence

Agriculture, 119; disadvantages of, 137; and government aid, 144; of Herero, 119, 120; ideology of, versus foraging, 137–138; transition to, 135–136

Alcohol, 148

See also Beer

Alternating generations, principle of, 63–64, 65

Amphibians, 23

Ancestors, ghosts of (see //gangwasi)

Animals, game, 23

See also Fauna; Hunting

Arrows, sharing of, 50; source of poison for, 25

Avoidance relationships, 64, 65, 66, 126; and marriage prohibitions, 75

Baby sling, 38f, 39

Baobab, 16, 43

Barnard, Alan, 11, 63n

Barter, 98

BaTawana, 121

Bate, 15

Beer, 140, 144

BaYei, 121

Biesele, Megan, 12n, 106n

Birds, game, 23

Blacks, 14, 15, 16; sorcery of, 103, 116–117

See also Herero; Tswana

Bleek, Dorothea, 11

Blurton-Jones, Nicholas, 12n

Bride service, 76, 77, 82

Brooks, Alison, 16, 33

Bush, returning to, 149

Bushmen, racist and sexist connotations of term, 9

Caloric consumption, 36, 54

Camps, 57–61; changes in, causes of, 60, 61; core of, 5–6, 58, 59, 60; evolution of, 58–61; flexibility of, 57, 58; layout of, 30–32; names of, 58; members of, number of, 57, 58, 60; "owners" of, 5–6, 58, 87–88

Carrying, 37–40; devices for, 35, 37–40; vocabulary of, 39, 40t, 42f

Carrying net, 38f, 39

Cashdan, Elizabeth, 11

Cattle (see Livestock production)

Chagnon, Napoleon, 149–150

Chapman, Thomas, 1

Children, and sexuality, 84; and school, 141–142; use of, in agriculture and herding, 137

Client groups, 57, 58, 124

Climate, 19, 25–27

Clothing, 3–4, 35, 37, 38f, 39f

Coal handling, 110

Conflict, 90–97; causes of, 93, 94t; and change in group composition, 60; and gift exchange, 101; handling, changes in, 96–97; and joking, 92; and laughter, 92, 93; levels of, as distinguished by !Kung, 92; and marriage, 77–79, 81–82, 84–85; and sexual jealousy, 86, 90; and violence, 90–97; and visiting, 101

See also Fighting; Homicide; Violence; Warfare, genocidal

Cooking pits, 31

Court, Tswana, 96–97, 121

Cousins, prohibitions on marriage to, 75

Craft marketing, 144

Dance(s), Drum, Women's, 15, 113–115; Giraffe, 80, 103, 109–113, 117; healing, 80, 103, 109–113, 117; Mine, 117; Trees, 117

Darwin, Charles, 33n, 92

Defecation, area of, 31–32

Dependency ratios, and changes in group composition, 60

DeVore, Irven, 1, 12, 18n

DeVore, Nancy, 1, 12n, 18n

Diet, animals in, 23, 24, 25; calories in, 36, 54; protein in, 54, and seasons, 25, 26, 27

See also specific food

Digging stick, 37, 38f

Divination, and hunting, 50

Divorce, 79

Dobe area, description of, 12–16; history of contact with, 9, 17–18; population of, by waterhole, 14, 15, 16

See also Environment

169